THE
ABUNDANT LIFE
OF

....

A 30-Week Devotional for
Mindfulness and Restoration

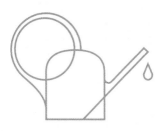

THE
ABUNDANT LIFE
JOURNAL

ANH LIN
Creator of Girl and the Word

Ink &
Willow

CONTENTS

A Letter from Anh

Dear friend,

It's a profound honor for me to share this intimate and inspirational devotional with you. Each page and activity is intentionally crafted to envelop you in peace, joy, and a deep connection to God's goodness. Think of this thirty-week journey as a walk with a close friend by your side, supporting you in your spiritual growth and healing.

I pray that the Spirit of God will go with you at every step, guiding you toward the abundant life designed uniquely for you. My hope is that when you reach the end of this study, you'll have found an increased sense of restoration and encouragement, regardless of your circumstances.

May the peace of God stand guard over your heart and mind as you navigate this beautiful journey toward abundance.

Warmest blessings,
Anh

Before You Begin

Take a few moments to reflect on where you are today and what you hope this experience will bring.

I started this journal on _____

At the end of my thirty-week journey, I hope to _____

_____

_____

These are the areas of my life I would like to improve:

1. _____

2. _____

3. _____

I hope that, with the help of this devotional journal, I will be able to...

1. _____

2. _____

3. _____

I want to believe that no matter what circumstances I'm facing,

_____

_____

I know that God has the best in store for me, so I will dedicate this season of my life to healing, growing, and thriving.

_____

Signature

ACCEPTANCE

Week 1
ACCEPTING YOURSELF

*I praise you because I am fearfully
and wonderfully made; your works are
wonderful, I know that full well.*

—Psalm 139:14, NIV

Would you say that you like yourself? That you accept yourself as you are? The journey to a genuine self-acceptance that encompasses the entirety of your being—mind, body, and spirit—is often void of glamour. Even though physical self-care is crucial, real self-acceptance means more than just buying fresh beauty products or acquiring new attire. True self-acceptance involves these aspects:

1. **Knowing who you are and whom you belong to.** You are a child of God. You are divine royalty, even if people have not treated you that way. Your identity is not determined by anyone except your Creator.

2. **Taking your thoughts captive.** In Christ, you have the power to capture every rebellious thought and teach it to obey him (2 Corinthians 10:5). Reflective journaling is a practical way of taking your thoughts captive.

3. **Fixing your eyes on what is good.** Whatever is true, honorable, right, pure, lovely, and admirable, think about such things (Philippians 4:8). Practice thinking these kinds of thoughts and speaking positively about yourself.

4. **Decluttering your priorities.** When any trace of godly wisdom is overshadowed with worries over prestige, image, wealth, or power, your soul becomes cluttered. Take some time this week to declutter your soul with the activities in the following pages.

Let's Pray Together

Dear heavenly Father, please teach me to take delight in things that are good. Show me how to be good to myself and tend to my soul when it cries out for more. May you remind me that I was made in your image. You are the most skilled potter, and I am your masterpiece. Thank you for giving me life! Your works are wonderful; I know that full well. In Jesus's name, amen.

You are only able to live in a way that really helps and loves others when your soul feels its worth.

—JOHN ORTBERG, *SOUL KEEPING*

Soul Care

What are three practical ways you can tend to your soul this week?
Express your answers with stickers,
illustrations, or short descriptions in the bubbles below.

Overcoming Negative Narratives

List five things your inner critic says about you on the left, and respond with what God says about you on the right.

WHAT YOUR INNER CRITIC SAYS	WHAT GOD SAYS
1.	1. ....
....	....
....	....
2.	2. ....
....	....
....	....
3.	3. ....
....	....
....	....
4.	4. ....
....	....
....	....
5.	5. ....
....	....
....	....

REFLECTION

What recurring negative thoughts does your inner critic often express, and how do these thoughts affect your daily life?

How can you actively invite God into your thought processes this week to help shift your focus from self-criticism to self-affirmation?

BRAIN DRAIN

Use this page to jot down any thoughts or feelings that might be taking up space in your mind this week.

Things to Do

Date: _____

- ○ ....
- ○ ....
- ○ ....

Date: _____

- ○ ....
- ○ ....
- ○ ....
- ○ ....

Date: _____

- ○ ....
- ○ ....
- ○ ....
- ○ ....

Date: _____

- ○ ....
- ○ ....
- ○ ....
- ○ ....

Date: _____

- ○ ....
- ○ ....
- ○ ....
- ○ ....

Date: _____

- ○ ....
- ○ ....
- ○ ....
- ○ ....

Date: _____

- ○ ....
- ○ ....
- ○ ....
- ○ ....

Week 2
ACCEPTING YOUR CIRCUMSTANCES

We know that God causes everything to work together for the good of those who love God and are called according to his purpose for them.

—Romans 8:28

If you are in a season of waiting, suffering, or spiritual dryness, keep in mind that God might be intentionally allowing you to go through it for the purpose of growing you. Even Jesus, who was God incarnate, spent the majority of his life as a carpenter. He laid aside all his rights as the Creator of humankind in order to be born in a dirty manger, live a humble life, and die a sinner's death on our behalf.

If you feel like you are in the wilderness right now, just know that Jesus deeply understands your suffering. Continue to pray, fast, and keep your eyes on your heavenly Father. The promise of a brighter tomorrow is on the horizon, whether here or in eternity, but remember that the next phase of your life requires significant inner growth—a sacred and intricate process that I often like to refer to as "heart work." May this time of introspection bring about profound transformation as you prepare for a new chapter.

Let's Pray Together

Dear heavenly Father, may you be my first thought when I wake up and my last thought before I sleep. Please surround me with your comforting presence and give me the peace that transcends all understanding. I pray that, in this season of waiting and suffering, you will soften my heart to your corrections, expose the wounds I never knew I had, and then heal them completely. In Jesus's name, amen.

Everything
will work out
for your good.

COLOR ME!

Serenity Prayer

List the things you would like to change in your life.

_____

_____

_____

_____

_____

*God grant me the serenity
To accept the things I cannot change;
Courage to change the things I can;
And wisdom to know the difference.
Living one day at a time;
Enjoying one moment at a time;
Accepting hardships as the pathway to peace;
Taking, as He did, this sinful world
As it is, not as I would have it;
Trusting that He will make all things right
If I surrender to His Will;
So that I may be reasonably happy in this life
And supremely happy with Him
Forever and ever in the next.
Amen.* *

* "The Serenity Prayer," Lords-Prayer-Words.com, accessed April 18, 2024, www.lords-prayer-words.com/famous_prayers/god_grant_me_the_serenity.html.

REFLECTION

Consider the concept of acceptance. Which aspects of your circumstances can you accept, and which do you find challenging to acknowledge or surrender?

Do you trust that God is in control of your life, even in difficult times? Why or why not?

BRAIN DRAIN

Use this page to jot down any thoughts or feelings that might be taking up space in your mind this week.

Things to Do

Date: _____

○ ....
○ ....
○ ....

Date: _____

○ ....
○ ....
○ ....
○ ....

Date: _____

○ ....
○ ....
○ ....
○ ....

Date: _____

○ ....
○ ....
○ ....
○ ....

Date: _____

○ ....
○ ....
○ ....
○ ....

Date: _____

○ ....
○ ....
○ ....
○ ....

Date: _____

○ ....
○ ....
○ ....
○ ....

Week 3
ACCEPTING OTHERS

Make allowance for each other's faults, and forgive anyone who offends you. Remember, the Lord forgave you, so you must forgive others. Above all, clothe yourselves with love, which binds us all together in perfect harmony.

—*Colossians 3:13–14*

We are usually hyperaware of the sins that we struggle with the most. As a result, when we see someone else (especially someone we care about) fall into the same sins, it reminds us of our own shortcomings and we end up getting angry with the person instead of the sin. There are four reasons it tends to be difficult for us to fully accept others when we think they've messed up:

1. **We don't think the person is deserving of forgiveness.**

2. **We are too distanced from them to empathize with their story.**

3. **We have extremely strong convictions against their lifestyle choices.**

4. **We secretly struggle with what they are outwardly embracing.**

It might be easy to antagonize someone after we've been hurt by them, but what if God did the same thing to us? If he kept a record of our wrongs, no one would stand a chance, because we are prone to making new mistakes every day. Forgiving others therefore helps us be grateful for our own forgiveness. The quality of our lives will also improve because—once we've extended forgiveness to others and accepted it for ourselves—the things that used to trigger us will no longer cause as much damage to our mental, emotional, and spiritual well-being.

Let's Pray Together

Dear heavenly Father, thank you for showing me undeserved grace. Out of all the ways you could have dealt with me when I was at my worst, you decided to win me over with kindness. Thank you for perfectly modeling love and forgiveness. I pray that you will take my heart of stone and give me a new heart of flesh. May you heal my deep-seated wounds so I can forgive those who have hurt me in the past. In Jesus's name, amen.

To be a
Christian means
to forgive the
inexcusable, because
God has forgiven
the inexcusable
in you.

—C. S. LEWIS, *THE WEIGHT OF GLORY*

Noting Your Triggers

List the qualities that tend to make you the most upset with other people. Remember, your triggers are your teachers.

Have you ever showcased the same qualities you just listed?
If so, circle the emotions you feel when you exert the same qualities
that frustrate you about others.

ANGER	CONFUSION	SADNESS	FEAR
Angry	Apprehensive	Apathetic	Afraid
Annoyed	Bewildered	Ashamed	Anxious
Defensive	Confused	Defeated	Cautious
Defiant	Discontent	Depressed	Cowardly
Disturbed	Disoriented	Despairing	Fearful
Exasperated	Distracted	Despondent	Helpless
Exploited	Exhausted	Discouraged	Insecure
Frustrated	Hesitant	Forlorn	Irrational
Furious	Impatient	Heartbroken	Panicked
Hateful	Obligated	Hopeless	Powerless
Hostile	Paralyzed	Hurt	Provoked
Intolerant	Perplexed	Inferior	Resentful
Irritated	Reluctant	Isolated	Shy
Mad	Surprised	Lonely	Skittish
Revengeful	Uncomfortable	Misunderstood	Suspicious
Stubborn	Uneasy	Mournful	Unsafe
Superior	Unsure	Overwhelmed	Worried

REFLECTION

*Reflect on any grudges you might be holding.
How is holding on to resentment affecting your well-being,
and what steps can you take to let go?*

*Think about a time when you were forgiven for an offense.
How did it feel to receive forgiveness, and how
can that experience guide you in forgiving others?*

BRAIN DRAIN

Use this page to jot down any thoughts or feelings that might be taking up space in your mind this week.

Things to Do

Date: _____

○ ....
○ ....
○ ....

Date: _____

○ ....
○ ....
○ ....
○ ....

Date: _____

○ ....
○ ....
○ ....

Date: _____

○ ....
○ ....
○ ....
○ ....

Date: _____

○ ....
○ ....
○ ....
○ ....

Date: _____

○ ....
○ ....
○ ....
○ ....

Date: _____

○ ....
○ ....
○ ....
○ ....

Week 4
ACCEPTING GOD

This is how God loved the world:
He gave his one and only Son, so that everyone
who believes in him will not perish
but have eternal life. God sent his Son into
the world not to judge the world, but to
save the world through him.

—*John 3:16–17*

It is crucial for us to observe the core characteristics of God and recognize those as truth over what we think we know about him apart from Scripture. Our feelings and experiences might not always be the best gauges for God's character. God is not flawed like us, with all our traumas, sins, and insecurities. He has no need to shout for our attention. He speaks to us with a still, small voice. He also does not force us to repent or to love him back. Instead, he chooses to love us with grace and shower us with kindness. The apostle Paul described God as being "wonderfully kind, tolerant, and patient" with us and observed that his kindness leads us to repentance (Romans 2:4). Accepting him is knowing that no matter what happens in life, we will be okay because we have a Father who loves and cares for us deeply. Everything is under his control, and his plans for us are good.

Let's Pray Together

Dear heavenly Father, thank you for sending your only Son to suffer and die on my behalf so I can have right standing with you despite my shortcomings. Thank you for making a way for me and for adopting me back into your family. I pray that you will soften my heart toward you so I can experience the fullness of joy and peace that comes from having a deeper relationship with you. I pray this in Jesus's name. Amen.

Describe the God you've rejected. Describe the God you don't believe in. Maybe I don't believe that God either.

—TIMOTHY KELLER*

* Timothy Keller (@timkellernyc), X, December 31, 2013, 4:11 P.M., https://x.com/timkellernyc/status/418142299345133569?lang=en.

The Imago Dei

Draw or use stickers to illustrate your idea of who God is.

This or That

*Check the answers that currently resonate with you more.
(Please remember that this exercise is simply to help you
identify your feelings. There are no right or wrong answers.)*

○ I feel safe when God and/or Jesus is mentioned.

○ I feel triggered when God and/or Jesus is mentioned.

○ I haven't worked through the hurt I've experienced.

○ I've begun working through the hurt I've experienced.

○ I want to grow closer to God.

○ I need a little more time to think about this.

○ I have a hard time trusting God.

○ I find it easy to trust God.

○ I feel confused as to why God has allowed bad things to happen to me.

○ I trust that God has a greater purpose for my suffering.

○ My experiences with other believers have a direct impact on my view of God.

○ I don't associate the behaviors of believers with the character of God.

○ I feel confused as to who God is.

○ I feel connected to who God is.

REFLECTION

*What preconceived notions or expectations
do you have about God?*

*How has this understanding been shaped by your experiences, and
does it closely align with how he reveals himself in Scripture?*

BRAIN DRAIN

*Use this page to jot down any thoughts or feelings that might
be taking up space in your mind this week.*

Things to Do

Date: _____

○ ....
○ ....
○ ....

Date: _____

○ ....
○ ....
○ ....
○ ....

Date: _____

○ ....
○ ....
○ ....
○ ....

Date: _____

○ ....
○ ....
○ ....
○ ....

Date: _____

○ ....
○ ....
○ ....
○ ....

Date: _____

○ ....
○ ....
○ ....
○ ....

Date: _____

○ ....
○ ....
○ ....
○ ....

PERSPECTIVE

Week 5
CHANGING YOUR PERSPECTIVE ON FAILURE

To keep me from becoming proud, I was given a thorn in my flesh, a messenger from Satan to torment me and keep me from becoming proud. Three different times I begged the Lord to take it away. Each time he said, "My grace is all you need. My power works best in weakness." So now I am glad to boast about my weaknesses, so that the power of Christ can work through me. That's why I take pleasure in my weaknesses, and in the insults, hardships, persecutions, and troubles that I suffer for Christ. For when I am weak, then I am strong.

—2 Corinthians 12:7–10

Many of us develop an unhealthy perspective on failure because we have suffered the serious consequences of it before. Certain failures hit harder than others, particularly the ones that are morally wrong and publicly criticized. The failures that are the most personal to us are often closely tied to our core identities.

To change your perspective on failure, you have to first detach your identity from your failures. No matter how big or complex your sins are, do not lose hope in God's love for you. His grace is extravagant enough to cover all your failures. He is eager to forgive you because he wants to give you a whole new identity rooted in him—an identity that is unshakable no matter your shortcomings.

Let's Pray Together

Dear heavenly Father, please wrap me in a loving embrace as I draw closer to you. I pray that you will heal my wounds from the consequences of my past failures. Help me forgive the people who were supposed to build me up during those times but instead shamed or punished me. May your Holy Spirit guide me as I learn how to change my perspective on failure and place my identity in you. In Jesus's name, amen.

Success is not final;
failure is not fatal.
It is the courage to
continue that counts.

I forgive myself for

The Art of Failing Forward

Failing does not make you a failure; it makes you human.
Here are some people who experienced years of defeat
but did not let it define them.

J. K. ROWLING

"I had failed on an epic scale. An exceptionally short-lived marriage had imploded, and I was jobless, a lone parent, and as poor as it is possible to be in modern Britain, without being homeless. The fears that my parents had had for me, and that I had had for myself, had both come to pass, and by every usual standard, I was the biggest failure I knew."[*]

Rowling went on to create the Harry Potter series, which has sold more than six hundred million copies worldwide and still holds the title as the bestselling series in history.

WALT DISNEY

"All the adversity I've had in my life, all my troubles and obstacles, have strengthened me. . . . You may not realize it when it happens, but a kick in the teeth may be the best thing in the world for you."[†]

* J. K. Rowling, "Text of J. K. Rowling's Speech," The Harvard Gazette, June 5, 2008, *https://news.harvard.edu/gazette/story/2008/06/text-of-j-k-rowling-speech.*
† Lewis Howes, "20 Lessons from Walt Disney on Entrepreneurship, Innovation and Chasing Your Dreams," Forbes, July 17, 2012, www.forbes.com/sites/lewishowes/2012/07/17/20-business-quotes-and-lessons-from-walt-disney.

Disney grew up in a low-income household with four siblings, under the watch of a domineering and allegedly abusive father. At the age of twenty-two, Disney was fired from a newspaper firm in Missouri, which cited a "lack of creativity" as the reason for letting him go.[‡] He continued on a rocky path toward success, failing at multiple ventures and accumulating millions in debt before finally establishing his ultra-successful animation studio and theme park.

MAYA ANGELOU

"'You may encounter many defeats, but you must not be defeated.' When you encounter defeats, you find out who you are, what you can rise up from."[§]

Angelou experienced abuse at a young age by her mother's boyfriend. Soon after she spoke up about this abuse, her abuser was found dead. Angelou became mute for the next five years because of the trauma and guilt. During that period of silence, she matured quickly and found her love for literature. Angelou went on to become one of America's most distinguished poets and civil rights activists.

‡ Olga Nesterova, "Walt Disney: Imagination Has No Age," Medium, January 3, 2024, *https://medium.com/@onestpreneur/walt-disney-imagination-has-no-age-dfb9a875598a*.
§ "You May Encounter Many Defeats, but You Must Not Be Defeated," Quote Investigator, July 3, 2023, https://quoteinvestigator.com/2023/07/03/not-defeated.

REFLECTION

In what ways have societal or cultural perceptions of failure influenced your own views?

Think about a recent setback. What alternative perspectives can you adopt to see it as a stepping stone rather than a roadblock?

BRAIN DRAIN

Use this page to jot down any thoughts or feelings that might be taking up space in your mind this week.

Things to Do

Date: _____

○ ....
○ ....
○ ....

Date: _____

○ ....
○ ....
○ ....
○ ....

Date: _____

○ ....
○ ....
○ ....
○ ....

Date: _____

○ ....
○ ....
○ ....
○ ....

Date: _____

○ ....
○ ....
○ ....
○ ....

Date: _____

○ ....
○ ....
○ ....
○ ....

Date: _____

○ ....
○ ....
○ ....
○ ....

Week 6
CHANGING YOUR
PERSPECTIVE ON SUCCESS

*True godliness with contentment
is itself great wealth.*

— *1 Timothy 6:6*

The definition of success varies from person to person, but that is okay. What matters most is that we learn how to separate our core identities from our achievements. This section will help you identify your goals and learn to find your worth and fulfillment in the Lord. But first, here are three foundational truths about success:

1. **Success is not always a destination, but it is always the result of a well-maintained life.** Think of it as completing a marathon rather than competing in a sprint.

2. **An evidence of success is lasting joy.** Success is not something on the horizon that you're constantly striving for. Success can always be found in the here and now, right where God has placed you. If you have joy, consider yourself already successful. Those who chase after the promise of success are really just chasing after lasting joy.

3. **Success is found in the ordinary.** You do not need to accomplish big things to gain more importance. You are already important. What is truly life-changing is learning to live with more consistency, integrity, and genuine love for others. These ordinary examples of faithfulness will produce much more joy, peace, and Christlikeness in you than any great feat ever could.

Let's Pray Together

Dear heavenly Father, thank you for revealing the insecurities I did not even know I had. Please remind me once again that your plans are so much more meaningful, fulfilling, and adventurous than anything I could ever dream of for myself. If there are any traces of impure motives in my heart when it comes to achieving success, may you sanctify those motives and introduce me to a sweeter way to live. Help me become a joyful, kind, and big-spirited person whose life will draw people to Jesus. In Jesus's name, amen.

This is what I need now: the courage to face an ordinary day...without despair; the bravery it takes to believe that a small life is still a meaningful life, and the grace to know that even when I've done nothing that is powerful or bold or even interesting that the Lord notices me and is fond of me and that that is enough.

—TISH HARRISON WARREN*

* Tish Harrison Warren, "Struggling with Everydayness," Renovaré, August 2021, http://renovare.org/articles/struggling-with-everydayness.

What Success Looks Like

What does success currently mean to you?
Draw or write your answers below.

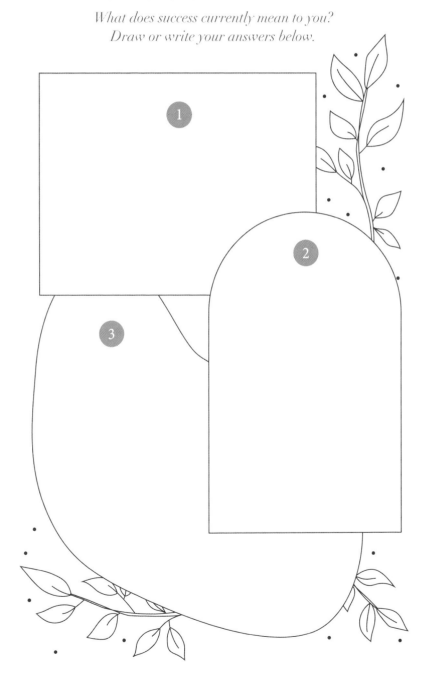

Book Recommendations

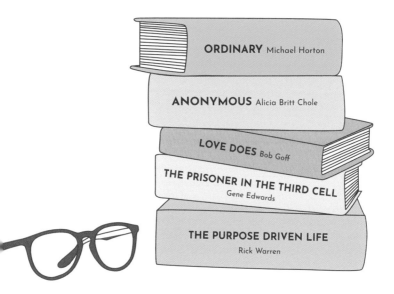

ORDINARY Michael Horton

ANONYMOUS Alicia Britt Chole

LOVE DOES Bob Goff

THE PRISONER IN THE THIRD CELL
Gene Edwards

THE PURPOSE DRIVEN LIFE
Rick Warren

Do you have any favorites of your own? List them below.

REFLECTION

*How do you want to be remembered by your children
(or future generations), and does your current pursuit of
success align with that vision?*

*In what ways can God's view of success be a source
of freedom and joy in your life?*

BRAIN DRAIN

Use this page to jot down any thoughts or feelings that might be taking up space in your mind this week.

Things to Do

Date: _____

○ ....
○ ....
○ ....

Date: _____

○ ....
○ ....
○ ....
○ ....

Date: _____

○ ....
○ ....
○ ....
○ ....

Date: _____

○ ....
○ ....
○ ....
○ ....

Date: _____

○ ....
○ ....
○ ....

Date: _____

○ ....
○ ....
○ ....
○ ....

Date: _____

○ ....
○ ....
○ ....
○ ....

Week 7
CHANGING YOUR
PERSPECTIVE ON HAPPINESS

Everything is wearisome beyond description. No matter how much we see, we are never satisfied. No matter how much we hear, we are not content.

—Ecclesiastes 1:8

You may have heard this common piece of advice: "Do what makes you happy." However, the emotion of happiness is entirely dictated by happenstance. In other words, what happens to you determines your level of happiness. The implications of this are serious. If your purpose is to be happy, you will find yourself craving only the peaks and dismissing the valleys. No one looks forward to the valleys, or seasons of suffering, but that is when you experience the most growth.

Happiness—which is fleeting and momentary—is not worthy to be your life's purpose. It is merely a product of your circumstances. Rather than chasing after happiness, allocate that energy to understanding your purpose. Once you discover your purpose, you will experience true joy, which is independent of your circumstances and will last through the peaks and valleys of your life. Nothing can take away your peace and joy when you know your purpose in Christ.

Let's Pray Together

Dear heavenly Father, I pray that you will show me how to put my hope in you so that no matter how dire my circumstances become, I can still have overwhelming peace in you. Thank you for promising to be with me through the storms. Please surround me with your comforting presence and walk with me all the days of my life. In Jesus's name, amen.

Happiness is fleeting and momentary. It's not worthy to be your life's purpose.

Glimmers of Joy

Fill this page with drawings, descriptions, or stickers of things that bring you great joy!

Sweet Middle Ground

*Fill in the Venn diagram with decisions that brought you
momentary happiness, lasting peace, or a combination of both.
You'll find that what brings you happiness isn't always best for
you and what brings you lasting peace isn't always fun at first.
Sometimes, though, there is a sweet middle ground where the
world's great needs align with your great joy!*

MOMENTARY
HAPPINESS

SWEET
MIDDLE
GROUND

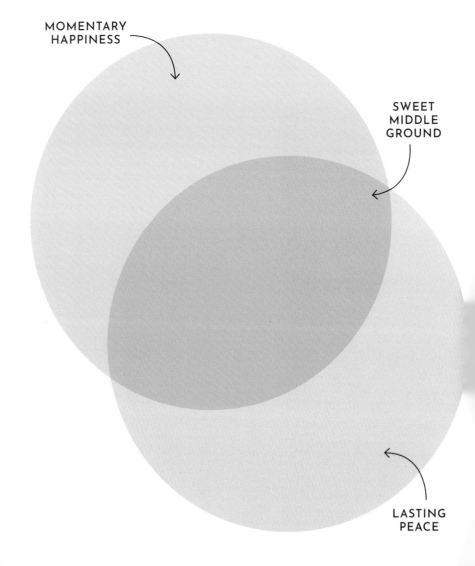

LASTING
PEACE

REFLECTION

How does being present in the moment contribute to your overall happiness?

What are your long-term goals? Do they align with biblical values and bring you joy, or are they driven by external expectations?

BRAIN DRAIN

Use this page to jot down any thoughts or feelings that might be taking up space in your mind this week.

Things to Do

Date: _____

- ○ ....
- ○ ....
- ○ ....

Date: _____

- ○ ....
- ○ ....
- ○ ....
- ○ ....

Date: _____

- ○ ....
- ○ ....
- ○ ....
- ○ ....

Date: _____

- ○ ....
- ○ ....
- ○ ....
- ○ ....

Date: _____

- ○ ....
- ○ ....
- ○ ....
- ○ ....

Date: _____

- ○ ....
- ○ ....
- ○ ....
- ○ ....

Week 8

CHANGING YOUR
PERSPECTIVE ON INTEGRITY

When you give a luncheon or dinner, do not invite your friends, your brothers or sisters, your relatives, or your rich neighbors; if you do, they may invite you back and so you will be repaid. But when you give a banquet, invite the poor, the crippled, the lame, the blind, and you will be blessed.

—*Luke 14:12–14, NIV*

Dictionary.com defines *integrity* as "the state of being whole and undivided."* When you develop a strong sense of integrity, you're able to follow through on promises, stand by your morals even when no one is looking, and create an inner life that truly reflects what you believe. To build your integrity, you can start by applying the following strategies:

1. **Identify the area where you lack integrity the most.**

2. **Practice breaking that habit daily.**

3. **Open up to at least one person you trust about this particular habit or struggle.**

4. **Avoid letting yourself be influenced by people who lack integrity.**

5. **Surround yourself with people who have outstanding integrity.**

Let's Pray Together

Dear heavenly Father, thank you for modeling integrity for me by following through on all your promises. I pray that as I try to pursue Christlike integrity, you will continue to encourage me with the joy of your presence. Create in me a new heart that yearns to be more like you, and help me surrender my old ways so I can live the abundant life you have always intended for me. In Jesus's name, amen.

---

* Oxfordlearnersdictionaries.com, s.v. "integrity," accessed July 8, 2024, www.oxfordlearnersdictionaries.com/us/definition/english/integrity.

Integrity

/in-te´-grə-tē/

(noun) The state of being whole and undivided

Integrity in Action

Describe a significant time when you've witnessed someone demonstrate their integrity. What impact did that event have on you?

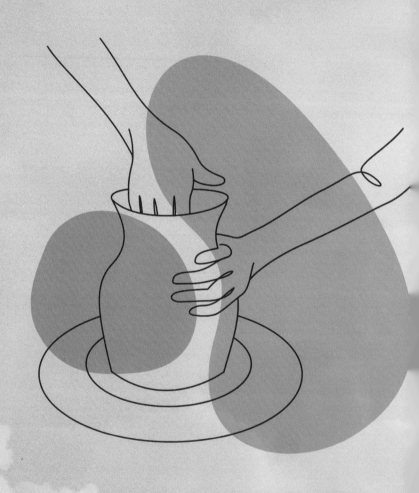

REFLECTION

In which areas do you lack integrity the most?

What practical steps will you take to break those habits?

BRAIN DRAIN

Use this page to jot down any thoughts or feelings that might be taking up space in your mind this week.

Things to Do

Date: _____

○ ....

○ ....

○ ....

Date: _____

○ ....

○ ....

○ ....

○ ....

Date: _____

○ ....

○ ....

○ ....

○ ....

Date: _____

○ ....

○ ....

○ ....

○ ....

Date: _____

○ ....

○ ....

○ ....

○ ....

Date: _____

○ ....

○ ....

○ ....

○ ....

Date: _____

○ ....

○ ....

○ ....

○ ....

IDENTITY

Week 9
CARVING OUT SPACE

This includes you who were once far away from God. You were his enemies, separated from him by your evil thoughts and actions. Yet now he has reconciled you to himself through the death of Christ in his physical body. As a result, he has brought you into his own presence, and you are holy and blameless as you stand before him without a single fault.

—Colossians 1:21–22

It is always worthwhile to carve out time to regroup and rediscover who we truly are. Different cultures teach us different things about our identities. For example, the general American culture teaches us that identity is self-created. On the other hand, Asian culture (at large) teaches that individual identities are bound to family and community. However, both of these worldviews lead to basing who we are on external things, such as our families, accomplishments, and careers.

The truth is, you are not simply a culmination of your experiences or of the people around you. Your identity was already given to you before you were even born. At your core, you are a child of God. This week, make time to sit in the fullness of your core identity, and witness how this profound awareness can influence every aspect of your life. Set aside fifteen to thirty minutes each day to meditate on this week's reflection verses and to journal and pray.

Let's Pray Together

Dear heavenly Father, thank you for calling me your beloved child. Thank you for giving me unmerited grace and a life that is meaningful and purpose driven. Please give me your wisdom and discernment as I seek to know the truth about my identity. May you also grant me the humility to accept this gift with open arms. In Jesus's name, amen.

It is better to move slowly with direction than to move quickly with good intentions.

Hold space for yourself to pause and reflect this week.

Breathing Exercise

Lean back in your chair.
Close your eyes.
Relax your shoulders.
Inhale through your nose for four counts.
Hold for four counts.
Exhale through your mouth for eight counts.
(Repeat three times.)

Patience Exercise

Connect the dots with smooth lines.

Note: Go slowly! Some dots double as two connection points.
(See answer on page 270.)

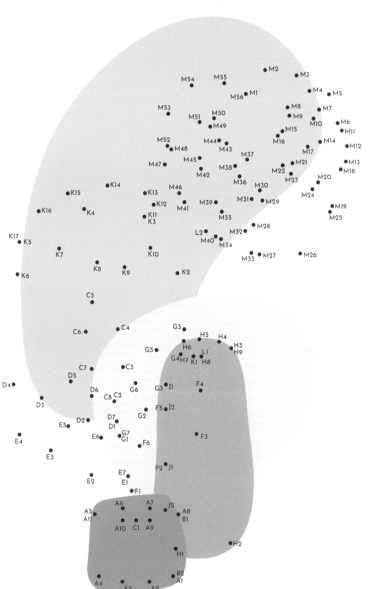

REFLECTION

How does it feel to know that God sees you as his holy and blameless child?

If you have a hard time believing that truth, what is holding you back from fully embracing your identity as a child of God?

BRAIN DRAIN

Use this page to jot down any thoughts or feelings that might be taking up space in your mind this week.

Things to Do

Date: _____

○ ....
○ ....
○ ....

Date: _____

○ ....
○ ....
○ ....
○ ....

Date: _____

○ ....
○ ....
○ ....

Date: _____

○ ....
○ ....
○ ....
○ ....

Date: _____

○ ....
○ ....
○ ....

Date: _____

○ ....
○ ....
○ ....
○ ....

Date: _____

○ ....
○ ....
○ ....
○ ....

Week 10
WHO YOU ARE NOT

All of us used to live that way, following the passionate desires and inclinations of our sinful nature. By our very nature we were subject to God's anger, just like everyone else. But God is so rich in mercy, and he loved us so much, that even though we were dead because of our sins, he gave us life when he raised Christ from the dead. (It is only by God's grace that you have been saved!)

—Ephesians 2:3–5

et's talk about the inner critic—that voice inside your head that is always self-critical and pessimistic. Your inner critic is formed by external factors, such as the opinions of your friends, family, and religious community or even different media channels. In contrast to what your inner critic says about you, here are some biblical truths about your identity:

1. **You are *not* what you do.** Your career, accomplishments, network, and social status do not make you any more or less valuable in the eyes of God.

2. **You are *not* what you possess.** From dust we were made, and to dust we will return (Genesis 3:19). Everything that we accumulate in this lifetime will remain on this side of heaven, so we should not put our identities in material possessions.

3. **You are *not* your physical appearance.** Genesis 1:27 tells us that we were made in the image of God (*imago Dei*). We should honor our bodies and take good care of them for the glory of God, but we should not worship our images.

Let's Pray Together

Dear heavenly Father, thank you for giving me an identity that is far more fulfilling than anything I can create for myself. Even though this world offers so many shiny promises, I pray that you will remind me that I am already loved and accepted by you. I pray that your Holy Spirit will always be louder than my inner critic. In Jesus's name, amen.

To be a Christian
does not mean
you were bad and
now you are good.
It means you were
dead and now you are
ALIVE!

Discover Who You Are

(See answer on page 270.)

```
K  D  M  I  C  V  R  I  N  F  I  B  F  B  D
D  P  E  F  M  E  O  E  I  E  N  E  R  J  E
S  I  G  I  S  A  T  G  Y  B  S  L  E  M  T
I  N  S  C  F  E  G  H  H  W  J  O  E  F  N
Y  U  U  D  L  I  T  O  P  C  M  V  H  T  A
F  E  T  P  V  R  T  A  D  A  D  E  A  C  W
D  A  M  T  O  E  Q  S  S  E  C  D  A  S  L
W  O  M  W  P  A  B  T  U  C  I  U  I  C  U
C  A  L  I  V  E  E  J  U  J  H  A  H  H  F
B  V  N  F  O  R  G  I  V  E  N  I  O  X  R
B  R  W  S  P  M  C  M  C  T  J  L  L  Y  E
I  Q  I  I  P  A  U  F  V  Y  Y  P  N  D  D
F  Z  E  U  C  D  E  H  S  I  R  E  H  C  N
I  C  N  Y  O  D  E  L  L  A  C  H  U  V  O
E  Y  B  U  D  Q  S  E  I  I  Y  P  Z  T  W
```

Words:

- ○ Alive
- ○ Beloved
- ○ Called
- ○ Cherished
- ○ Child
- ○ Chosen
- ○ Complete
- ○ Forgiven
- ○ Free
- ○ Holy
- ○ Imago Dei
- ○ Justified
- ○ Masterpiece
- ○ Rescued
- ○ Wanted
- ○ Wonderful
- ○ Worthy

Expectations Versus Truth

List five things society expects of you on the left, and respond with who God says you are on the right.

Example: *Society says my worth is determined by my wealth. God says I am already infinitely worthy.*

SOCIETAL EXPECTATIONS	YOUR GOD-GIVEN IDENTITY
1.	1. ....
2.	2. ....
3.	3. ....
4.	4. ....
5.	5. ....

REFLECTION

*What labels or identities have others placed on you
that don't align with your identity in Christ?*

*How can you let go of these external definitions and
fully embrace your identity as a child of God?*

BRAIN DRAIN

Use this page to jot down any thoughts or feelings that might be taking up space in your mind this week.

Things to Do

Date: _____

○ ....

○ ....

○ ....

Date: _____

○ ....

○ ....

○ ....

○ ....

Date: _____

○ ....

○ ....

○ ....

○ ....

Date: _____

○ ....

○ ....

○ ....

○ ....

Date: _____

○ ....

○ ....

○ ....

○ ....

Date: _____

○ ....

○ ....

○ ....

○ ....

Date: _____

○ ....

○ ....

○ ....

○ ....

Week 11
A GIVEN IDENTITY

Anyone who belongs to Christ has become a new person. The old life is gone; a new life has begun!

—2 Corinthians 5:17

dentity and self-worth are not meant to be self-created. The theologian Martin Luther once said, "God doesn't love us because of our worth; we are of worth because God loves us."* This biblical philosophy means that you are worthy without having to prove your worth, because your Creator has already deemed you worthy. You are a child of God—not because of anything you have done but because of his choice to redeem and adopt you as his own. You are loved without even having to earn it, because the Father's love for you is unconditional.

Any love that has to be earned is not going to last forever, but your identity is built on a love that endures through all things—especially through your shortcomings. This week, we will explore how you can lean into your given identity as a beloved child of God.

Let's Pray Together

Dear heavenly Father, I praise you for loving me before I was even brought into existence. I pray that you will empower me to embrace my given worth and identity as your beloved child. When I am feeling defeated, remind me that you are always for me. Please help me experience your perfect love like never before. In Jesus's name, amen.

* "God Doesn't Love Us Because of Our Worth, We Are of Worth Because God Loves Us." Grace Quotes, accessed April 18, 2024, https://gracequotes.org/quote/god-doesnt-love-us-because-of-our-worth-we-are-of-worth-because-god-loves-us.

Origami Stars

Your identity as a child of God is a gift, not a reward.
It cannot be earned, only received.

Cut out the strips on the next page to create beautiful origami stars to place in a jar. Just as each one is unique and lovely in its own way, so are you in the eyes of God!

1 Make a loop at one end of the paper. Weave the short end of the paper through the loop.

2 Tighten the knot and press it flat.

3 Fold the short end of the paper down toward the center of the star. If it is too long, tear off a small piece.

4 Fold the long end of the paper over the edges of the knot until it becomes a pentagon.

5 Keep folding the long end of the paper until it is too short to continue. Tuck the leftover paper under the nearest layer.

6 Hold the pentagon by the edges as if you were holding a coin. Use your fingernail to press in one of the edges. Rotate the pentagon and press again until all five sides have been pressed.

REFLECTION

What does being a child of God mean to you personally?

How can you reinforce and internalize the truth about your given identity in Christ?

BRAIN DRAIN

Use this page to jot down any thoughts or feelings that might be taking up space in your mind this week.

Things to Do

Date: _____

- ○ ....
- ○ ....
- ○ ....

Date: _____

- ○ ....
- ○ ....
- ○ ....
- ○ ....

Date: _____

- ○ ....
- ○ ....
- ○ ....
- ○ ....

Date: _____

- ○ ....
- ○ ....
- ○ ....
- ○ ....

Date: _____

- ○ ....
- ○ ....
- ○ ....
- ○ ....

Date: _____

- ○ ....
- ○ ....
- ○ ....
- ○ ....

Date: _____

- ○ ....
- ○ ....
- ○ ....
- ○ ....

Week 12
LIVING IT OUT

We can rejoice, too, when we run into problems and trials, for we know that they help us develop endurance. And endurance develops strength of character, and character strengthens our confident hope of salvation. And this hope will not lead to disappointment. For we know how dearly God loves us, because he has given us the Holy Spirit to fill our hearts with his love.

—Romans 5:3–5

When our identities are attached to people, accolades, or material things, we run the risk of losing ourselves if those things are ever taken away from us. People often feel the depths of hopelessness after they have lost the person or thing that is most valuable to them, not knowing that they had subconsciously merged their identity with that person or thing. On the flip side, if you place your identity in Jesus instead, you belong to him and him alone—not to the temporal things of this world. When your identity is firmly placed in Jesus, you will have hope no matter how dire your circumstances seem. You will also be able to trust that both the good and the bad are ultimately part of God's plan and that he truly cares about the condition of your soul.

Let's Pray Together

Dear heavenly Father, I know that my trials are your mercies in disguise. Through my fellowship with you in suffering, help me develop endurance, strength of character, and more confidence in your faithfulness. I pray that you will shape me each day to look more like your Son, Jesus. May my heart truly begin to reflect yours. In Jesus's name, amen.

What matters is not the accomplishments you achieve; what matters is the person you become.

–DALLAS WILLARD

Embracing the New

Set aside some time this week to embark on something new.
You can try a new DIY project or even cook up a new recipe!
Here are a couple of my favorite easy-to-make snacks:

AVOCADO FRIES

Ingredients

- 2 large not-too-ripe avocados
- ½ teaspoon garlic salt
- ¼ teaspoon pepper
- ¼ cup flour
- 1 egg, lightly beaten
- 1 cup panko breadcrumbs
- A drizzle of olive oil (or another cooking oil)
- Honey mustard (or your favorite dip)

Instructions

1. Preheat the oven to 400°F, and oil your baking tray.

2. Cut your avocados into thick slices, and season with garlic salt and pepper.

3. Dip your avocado slices in the flour, egg, and panko breadcrumbs (in that order). Make sure to coat each piece evenly.

4. Set the coated pieces on the baking tray. Drizzle with olive oil, and bake for 15 minutes (or until the avocado fries turn golden).

5. Let the fries cool, and then enjoy them with your favorite dipping sauce!

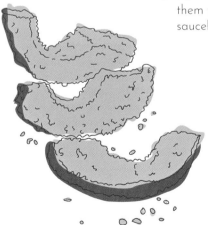

BLUEBERRY GALETTES

Ingredients

Crust

2½ cups all-purpose flour

1 tablespoon granulated sugar

1 teaspoon salt

4 tablespoons ice water

1 cup unsalted butter, cold and cut into cubes

Filling

⅓ cup granulated sugar

2 tablespoons cornstarch

¼ teaspoon freshly ground nutmeg

Zest of 1 lemon

1½ cups fresh blueberries

Assembly

1 egg for egg wash

Coarse sugar for sprinkling

Instructions

1. Preheat the oven to 400°F, and line a sheet pan with parchment paper.

2. For the crust, combine the flour, sugar, and salt in a mixing bowl. Add the ice water and butter, and mix until evenly combined. Then refrigerate for 20 minutes.

3. For the filling, combine the sugar, cornstarch, nutmeg, and lemon zest in a bowl. Add the blueberries, and toss to coat. Set aside.

4. Divide the dough into three equal sections, and roll it out into three 8"-10" flat disks. They don't need to be exact or even. Scoop 4-6 tablespoons of the blueberry filling into the center of each disk, and fold the dough over the edge of the filling in a circular shape.

5. Brush the dough with egg wash, and sprinkle with granulated sugar.

6. Bake for 30-35 minutes or until the crust is golden and the filling is bubbling.

7. Serve warm or at room temperature. Store galettes in the fridge for up to 4 days.

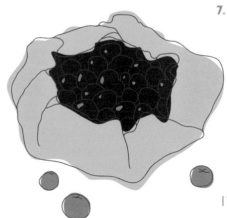

REFLECTION

How does your understanding of being a child of God motivate you in your personal goals or in your relationships with others?

Are there specific challenges or joys you've experienced in connecting with others through your identity in Christ?

BRAIN DRAIN

Use this page to jot down any thoughts or feelings that might be taking up space in your mind this week.

Things to Do

Date: _____

○ ....
○ ....
○ ....

Date: _____

○ ....
○ ....
○ ....
○ ....

Date: _____

○ ....
○ ....
○ ....
○ ....

Date: _____

○ ....
○ ....
○ ....
○ ....

Date: _____

○ ....
○ ....
○ ....
○ ....

Date: _____

○ ....
○ ....
○ ....
○ ....

Date: _____

○ ....
○ ....
○ ....
○ ....

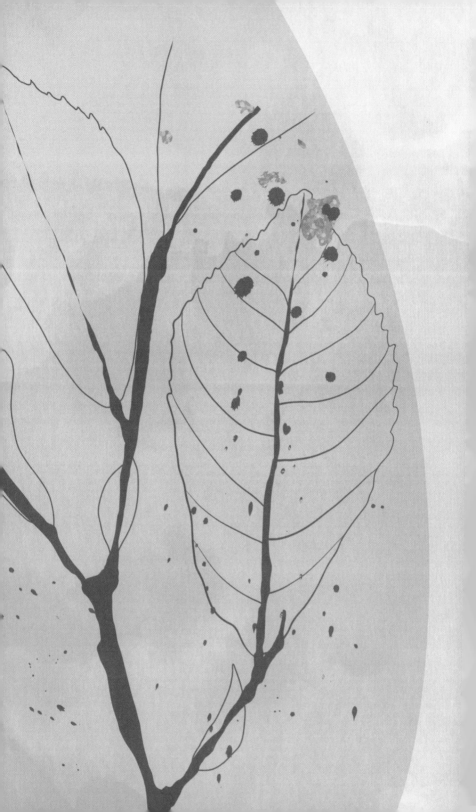

PURPOSE

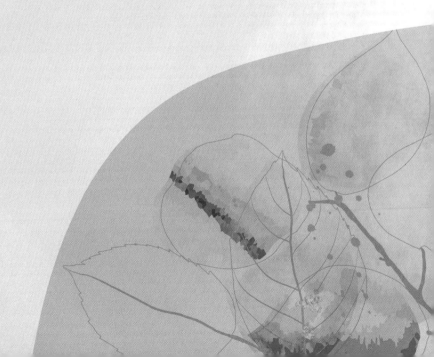

Week 13
EMBRACING YOUR PURPOSE

Jesus stood and shouted to the crowds, "Anyone who is thirsty may come to me! Anyone who believes in me may come and drink! For the Scriptures declare, 'Rivers of living water will flow from his heart.'"

—John 7:37–38

Many people go through life with the sole purpose of maximizing their pleasures while minimizing their pain. Although it is not wrong to want a happy and pleasurable life, our purpose should be neither self-created nor purely self-serving.

The purpose of an object is determined by its creator. Similarly, as creations of a divine Creator, our true purpose is rooted in him. When we seek purpose apart from our Creator, we often find ourselves chasing after things that can never truly fulfill us. While blessings like family, financial stability, and success are important, they cannot satisfy our deepest longing for purpose.

Our true purpose encompasses three dimensions: spiritual, physical, and vocational. For the next few weeks, we will explore this tri-fold purpose to help you live a more intentional and fulfilling life.

Let's Pray Together

Dear heavenly Father, please give me divine discernment so I can discover my true purpose in life. No matter how busy, hectic, painful, or disappointing life can be, I pray that I will never lose sight of the greater purpose you have given me. May you lead me toward the path that is most pleasing to you. In Jesus's name, amen.

Our purpose is tri-fold:

VOCATIONAL

PHYSICAL

SPIRITUAL

Your Tri-Fold Purpose

Without reading ahead, try to define your current spiritual, physical, and vocational purposes. If you do not have a sure answer yet, simply fill in the blanks with what you think each purpose means. We will revisit these answers at the end of the Purpose section.

My spiritual purpose is _____

_____

_____

_____

_____

My physical purpose is _____

_____

_____

_____

_____

My vocational purpose is _____

_____

_____

_____

_____

Finding your tri-fold purpose can feel a lot like navigating
through a complex maze—it takes patience, faith, and
quite a few tries. In the maze below, use a pencil
to trace your way toward true purpose!

(See answer on page 270.)

Start here!

PURPOSE

REFLECTION

*With total transparency and honesty, what has been
your life's purpose up until this point?*

*Have challenges or obstacles made you question your
purpose in Christ? If so, what were those challenges?*

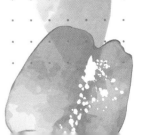

BRAIN DRAIN

Use this page to jot down any thoughts or feelings that might be taking up space in your mind this week.

Things to Do

Date: _____

○ ....

○ ....

○ ....

Date: _____

○ ....

○ ....

○ ....

○ ....

Date: _____

○ ....

○ ....

○ ....

○ ....

Date: _____

○ ....

○ ....

○ ....

○ ....

Date: _____

○ ....

○ ....

○ ....

○ ....

Date: _____

○ ....

○ ....

○ ....

○ ....

Date: _____

○ ....

○ ....

○ ....

○ ....

Week 14
YOUR SPIRITUAL PURPOSE

The twenty-four elders fall down and worship the one sitting on the throne (the one who lives forever and ever). And they lay their crowns before the throne and say, "You are worthy, O Lord our God, to receive glory and honor and power. For you created all things, and they exist because you created what you pleased."

—*Revelation 4:10–11*

All the layers of your tri-fold purpose are tied together, making sense of one another. There cannot be a vocational purpose without a physical purpose, or a physical purpose without a spiritual purpose. As important as they all are, consider your spiritual purpose as the foundation underlying all your actions. Before you start *doing*, you have to learn how to *be*.

To put it simply, your spiritual purpose is to be loved by God. To some, "being loved" hardly sounds like a purpose at all. It does not involve you doing anything to earn that love. Yet an object does not define its own purpose; it receives purpose from its creator. Merely existing as a person whom God loves is inherently purposeful, and embracing this love is your initial stride toward complete fulfillment.

Let's Pray Together

Dear heavenly Father, thank you for creating me because you loved the thought of my existence. You breathed your own breath into my lungs—what an intimate and humbling way to create life! Thank you for being my heavenly Father, Creator, and Friend. You are a good king—the King of kings. And to you, all of heaven falls down in worship because you created all things. They exist only because you created what brought you great pleasure. Help me embrace that truth no matter what tribulations may come my way. In Jesus's name, amen.

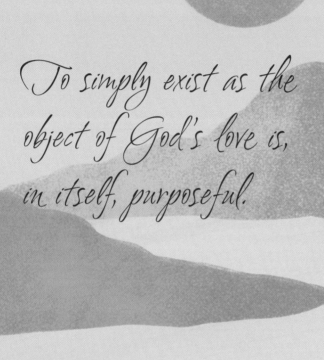

To simply exist as the
object of God's love is,
in itself, purposeful.

COLOR ME!

God rejoices in his works because his works are an expression of his glory.

—JOHN PIPER

Even good things can feel empty when they do not serve a spiritual purpose. Write down three things you enjoy doing and how they contribute toward a spiritual purpose in your life.

Example: *Singing—using my God-given talent— brings me joy and makes me feel closer to God.*

1. _____

Its spiritual purpose

_____

_____

_____

2. _____

Its spiritual purpose

_____

_____

_____

3. _____

Its spiritual purpose

_____

_____

_____

REFLECTION

Is there any part of you that does not believe you were created to be loved by God? Why is that?

How can you actively seek God's guidance when discerning your purpose rather than relying only on personal reflection?

BRAIN DRAIN

Use this page to jot down any thoughts or feelings that might be taking up space in your mind this week.

Things to Do

Date: _____

○ ....
○ ....
○ ....

Date: _____

○ ....
○ ....
○ ....
○ ....

Date: _____

○ ....
○ ....
○ ....
○ ....

Date: _____

○ ....
○ ....
○ ....
○ ....

Date: _____

○ ....
○ ....
○ ....
○ ....

Date: _____

○ ....
○ ....
○ ....
○ ....

Date: _____

○ ....
○ ....
○ ....
○ ....

Week 15
YOUR PHYSICAL PURPOSE

God has given each of you a gift from his great variety of spiritual gifts. Use them well to serve one another. Do you have the gift of speaking? Then speak as though God himself were speaking through you. Do you have the gift of helping others? Do it with all the strength and energy that God supplies. Then everything you do will bring glory to God through Jesus Christ. All glory and power to him forever and ever! Amen.

—1 Peter 4:10–11

Ever since the creation of Adam and Eve in the Garden of Eden, our God-given task has been to "fill the earth and subdue it" (Genesis 1:28, NIV). This directive, in part, refers to populating the earth with fellow image-bearers of God while responsibly managing its resources. But what if having biological children is not an option for you? Issues like infertility, singleness, financial lack, and illness have certainly marked our world since the time of Abraham. Thankfully, the "fill the earth" part of our purpose is not restricted to bearing children. Whatever your situation in life, you can still fulfill this aspect of our physical purpose by sharing your faith with others and by raising up and nurturing spiritual daughters and sons.

The second facet of our physical purpose refers to exercising dominion over the earth. Although the presence of sin and the reality of a fallen world has led to environmental degradation, we're still tasked with stewarding creation to honor God. Whether through simple acts like recycling or larger endeavors such as advancing eco-friendly technology, our responsibility is clear: to cultivate a planet that brings glory to its Creator.

Let's Pray Together

Dear heavenly Father, thank you for equipping me with the intelligence and motivation needed to fulfill my physical purpose. I pray for all the women who have dealt with infertility or otherwise have not been able to bear children. Please hold them close to you and give them comfort. May you also give me the wisdom to fulfill my physical purpose in a way that pleases you. In Jesus's name, amen.

Living Fruitfully

*List the practical ways in which you can
"be fruitful and multiply" (Genesis 1:28).*

How I Steward the Earth
BINGO CHALLENGE

Challenge yourself to complete a full bingo sequence this month!

RECYCLE	THRIFT	COMPOST	PLANT A TREE	REDUCE PLASTIC USE
CONSERVE WATER	USE LED LIGHTBULBS	BUY REUSABLE DRYER BALLS	BIKE TO WORK	BUY SUSTAINABLE BRANDS
AVOID LITTERING	USE BIO-DEGRADABLE TO-GO CONTAINERS	FREE ♻	GO PAPERLESS	SHARE A RIDE
SWITCH TO A REUSABLE WATER BOTTLE	START A GARDEN	TAKE PUBLIC TRANS-PORTATION	SHOP WITH A REUSABLE TOTE	DONATE OLD THINGS
SWITCH TO A REUSABLE STRAW	ATTEND A TEAM CLEANUP	BUY WASHABLE KITCHEN NAPKINS	USE ECO-FRIENDLY FOOD WRAP	BUY BULK INGREDIENT

REFLECTION

*What changes can you make in your life to live out
your physical purpose this week?*

What kind of impact do you hope your life's purpose will have?

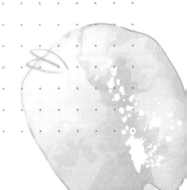

BRAIN DRAIN

Use this page to jot down any thoughts or feelings that might be taking up space in your mind this week.

Things to Do

Date: _____

○ ....

○ ....

○ ....

Date: _____

○ ....

○ ....

○ ....

○ ....

Date: _____

○ ....

○ ....

○ ....

○ ....

Date: _____

○ ....

○ ....

○ ....

○ ....

Date: _____

○ ....

○ ....

○ ....

○ ....

Date: _____

○ ....

○ ....

○ ....

○ ....

Date: _____

○ ....

○ ....

○ ....

○ ....

Week 16
YOUR VOCATIONAL PURPOSE

*Whether you eat or drink or whatever you do, do
it all for the glory of God. Do not cause anyone
to stumble, whether Jews, Greeks or the church
of God—even as I try to please everyone in every
way. For I am not seeking my own good but the
good of many, so that they may be saved.*

—1 Corinthians 10:31–33, NIV

Your vocation extends beyond any traditional career path and encompasses any primary role or responsibility entrusted to you by the Lord—be it full-time parenting or overseas missions. While this vocational calling is important, it should come after our spiritual and physical purposes in terms of priority. Yet for some reason, we tend to think of "jobs" and "careers" first when someone brings up the topic of purpose.

Still, discerning the "why" behind your job is just as crucial as the role itself. Because God assigns various roles—often seasonally—you don't have to feel as though you are trapped in the same vocational calling forever. Instead, think of your vocation right now as your assignment in this particular season of life. This mindset will help you hold fast to your divine purpose in the workplace without placing your identity *in* your assignment. Recognizing that your current position is for God's glory, and not for personal gain, can help transform even the simplest tasks into ones with eternal significance. As Timothy Keller wisely stated, "Every good endeavor, even the simplest ones, pursued in response to God's calling, can matter forever."*

Let's Pray Together

Dear heavenly Father, thank you for giving me a deeper reason to do the work I have to do on the earth. Thank you for allowing me to worship you even in the simplest ways, such as doing chores and running errands. With you at the center of my purpose, may my work become a means to bless others and bring glory to your name. In Jesus's name, amen.

* Timothy Keller, *Every Good Endeavor: Connecting Your Work to God's Work* (New York: Penguin Books, 2016), 14.

You don't do good to be saved, but you are saved to do good.

—THOMAS KANG

Careers by Enneagram

Take the Enneagram test at EnneagramInstitute.com. The vocations below might be suitable to your Enneagram type. Remember, you are never limited to lists! This is simply to help you get started on thinking about some options.[*]

TYPE	IDEAL CAREER PATHS	CORE NEEDS
TYPE 1 **The Reformer**	Accountant Attorney Financial Planner Manager or Executive Publisher Scientist	Accountability and Responsibility
TYPE 2 **The Helper**	Ministry Worker Nonprofit Worker Nurse Social Worker Teacher Therapist	Genuine Connection and Appreciation
TYPE 3 **The Achiever**	Actor Brand Ambassador Entrepreneur Journalist Marketing Manager Motivational Speaker	Recognition and Reward

* Lists pulled from Lily Yuan, "Enneagram Careers Guide," Personality Psychology, accessed March 30, 2024, *http://personality-psychology.com/personality-psychology-resources/enneagram-careers -guide*; Coley Lane Bouschet, "What Career Path Is Best for You Based on Your Enneagram Type," Life Goals, accessed March 30, 2024, *http://lifegoalsmag.com/career-path-enneagram-type*; and Judith Akoyi, "Best Careers for Your Enneagram Type: Find the Right Job Based on Enneagram," BrainManager.io, April 13, 2023, *http://brainmanager.io/blog/career/best-careers-for-your-enneagram -type*.

TYPE	IDEAL CAREER PATHS	CORE NEEDS
TYPE 4 The Individualist	Artist Creative Writer Designer Filmmaker Photographer Songwriter	Creative Freedom and Flexibility
TYPE 5 The Investigator	Architect Author Computer Programmer Data Scientist Researcher Technical Writer	Autonomy and Exploration
TYPE 6 The Loyalist	Auditor Engineer Financial Adviser Police Officer Teacher Veterinarian	Security and Stability
TYPE 7 The Enthusiast	Event Planner Flight Attendant Life Coach Publicist Social Media Influencer Television/Podcast Host	Variety and Excitement

TYPE	IDEAL CAREER PATHS	CORE NEEDS
TYPE 8 **The Challenger**	Attorney Business Consultant Investor Marketing Strategist Politician Sales Director	Competence and Influence
TYPE 9 **The Peacemaker**	Counselor Editor Human Resources Manager Ministry Worker Social Worker Teacher	Harmony and Peace

REFLECTION

*Is it currently difficult for you to do your job for the glory of God?
Why or why not?*

*What are some untapped opportunities for you to make a
positive impact in areas outside your job description?*

BRAIN DRAIN

*Use this page to jot down any thoughts or feelings that might
be taking up space in your mind this week.*

Things to Do

Date: _____

○ ....

○ ....

○ ....

Date: _____

○ ....

○ ....

○ ....

○ ....

Date: _____

○ ....

○ ....

○ ....

○ ....

Date: _____

○ ....

○ ....

○ ....

○ ....

Date: _____

○ ....

○ ....

○ ....

○ ....

Date: _____

○ ....

○ ....

○ ....

○ ....

Week 17
LIVING PURPOSEFULLY

*In him all things were created: things in heaven
and on earth, visible and invisible, whether
thrones or powers or rulers or authorities; all
things have been created through him and for him.*

— *Colossians 1:16, NIV*

Our purpose is not about us. Rick Warren, the author of *The Purpose Driven Life*, began his book with the statement "It's not about you."[*] He continued, "The purpose of your life is far greater than your own personal fulfillment, your peace of mind, or even your happiness. It's far greater than your family, your career, or even your wildest dreams and ambitions. If you want to know why you were placed on this planet, you must begin with God. You were born *by* his purpose and *for* his purpose."

The whole point of finding your purpose is not so that you will have more recognition, wealth, or prestige but so that you will become more effective and joyful in life, doing exactly what you were made to do. As the Scriptures say in Colossians 1:16, you were made *by* him and *for* him.

Let's Pray Together

Dear heavenly Father, thank you for assigning each and every one of us such significant roles in your grand plan. Even if I don't see the significance of my job at the moment, I pray that you will still remind me of how I was made for your special purposes. I know that you can use all things to bring about your incredible plans. Please help me rely on the Holy Spirit's guidance every step of the way. In Jesus's name, amen.

* Rick Warren, *The Purpose Driven Life: What on Earth Am I Here For?*, rev. ed. (Grand Rapids, Mich.: Zondervan, 2012), 21.

Your Renewed Purpose

*Now that you've learned about your tri-fold purpose,
fill out an updated version of what you wrote on page 119.
Do you notice any significant changes?*

My spiritual purpose is _____

_____

_____

_____

_____

My physical purpose is _____

_____

_____

_____

_____

My vocational purpose is _____

_____

_____

_____

_____

Ten Points on What It Looks Like to Live a Purpose-Driven Life

1. You have a deep appreciation of God's immense love for you.

2. You know that his love is based not on what you have accomplished but on the fact that you are his beloved child.

3. From the overflow of that love, you yearn to live out his purpose for you by being a good steward of the world he has given you.

4. You want to make a positive impact on the world—not because it will bring you recognition but because you want to love the people in it.

5. No matter what job you are given in this season, you are determined to do it with joy and intention because it is for the glory of God.

6. You understand that there is always a deeper reason when God brings you through trials.

7. Even through seasons of suffering, you surrender your pain to the Lord and push forward with confidence.

8. You firmly understand that your life is about service to others, not just yourself.

9. Even in the vague seasons, when God seems to go silent and offer no clear signs, you are still willing to wait on the Lord before making any permanent decisions.

10. You are in constant communication with the Lord, acknowledging his presence and activity in your daily life.

REFLECTION

Which point on the previous page resonates with you the most? Why?

Which do you need to work on the most, and how will you go about doing that?

BRAIN DRAIN

Use this page to jot down any thoughts or feelings that might be taking up space in your mind this week.

Things to Do

Date: _____
- ○ ....
- ○ ....
- ○ ....

Date: _____
- ○ ....
- ○ ....
- ○ ....
- ○ ....

Date: _____
- ○ ....
- ○ ....
- ○ ....
- ○ ....

Date: _____
- ○ ....
- ○ ....
- ○ ....
- ○ ....

Date: _____
- ○ ....
- ○ ....
- ○ ....
- ○ ....

Date: _____
- ○ ....
- ○ ....
- ○ ....
- ○ ....

Date: _____
- ○ ....
- ○ ....
- ○ ....
- ○ ....

BOUNDARIES

Week 18
BOUNDARIES DEFINED

Lord, you alone are my inheritance, my cup of blessing. You guard all that is mine. The land you have given me is a pleasant land. What a wonderful inheritance! I will bless the Lord who guides me; even at night my heart instructs me. I know the Lord is always with me. I will not be shaken, for he is right beside me. No wonder my heart is glad, and I rejoice. My body rests in safety.

—Psalm 16:5–9

Those who have a boundary problem do not usually know it. This is why they tend to repeat the same destructive behaviors and get stuck in a loop of unhealthy patterns. It is not their fault, but it is their responsibility to change these unhealthy habits and learn new ways of approaching life.

Our boundaries are supposed to be like fences that keep the good in and the bad out. However, unhealthy boundaries trap the bad inside and keep the good outside. They no longer act like fences but are impenetrable walls. If this sounds familiar to you, this section will help you identify signs of unhealthy boundaries and rebuild them in a way that lets you heal and thrive.

Let's Pray Together

Dear heavenly Father, thank you for demonstrating what it means to have good boundaries. You have clearly communicated your likes and dislikes and the consequences of trespassing your boundaries. I pray that you will teach me to have the same self-respect and confidence that you have, knowing that I am your beloved child. I want to reflect you in every way. May this section be the push I need to live a boundary-ful, joyful, and abundant life. In Jesus's name, amen.

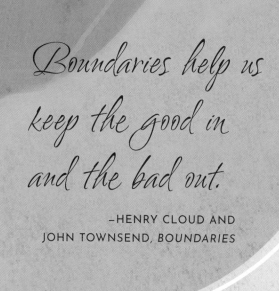

Boundaries help us keep the good in and the bad out.

—HENRY CLOUD AND
JOHN TOWNSEND, *BOUNDARIES*

Boundary Types

Here are eight prominent examples of boundaries, adapted from the book Boundaries *by Henry Cloud and John Townsend.* *

1. **Skin**

   Not only does your skin act as a fence between your internal organs and the outside world, but it is also the most basic boundary line. As Cloud and Townsend explain, "Victims of physical and sexual abuse often have a poor sense of boundaries. Early in life they were taught that their property did not really begin at their skin."

2. **Words**

   As a child, your most basic boundary-setting skill was to say *no*. Vocalizing your boundaries lets people know you are not an extension of them but an individual with your own tastes and preferences. Saying no also communicates that you are responsible for only yourself.

3. **Truth**

   Adhering to the Lord's spiritual boundaries will help you make sense of your intrinsic worth, your inherent beauty, and your purpose on earth.

4. **Geographical distance**

   This form of boundary setting physically removes you from the situation. Sometimes it is necessary to create a safe space so you can maintain a calm and sound mind.

* Henry Cloud and John Townsend, *Boundaries: When to Say Yes, How to Say No to Take Control of Your Life*, rev. ed. (Grand Rapids, Mich.: Zondervan, 2017), 35–40.

5. **Time**

Taking time apart from your stressor allows you to regroup mentally and emotionally. Giving yourself time helps you regain "ownership over some out-of-control aspect of your life where boundaries need to be set." You are literally giving yourself a time-out to breathe and think more clearly.

6. **Emotional distance**

Everyone experiences emotional distancing at some point, but this should not be a permanent way of living. By emotionally distancing yourself from someone or something, you are temporarily protecting yourself from further harm. However, emotions must always be addressed and worked out thoroughly for you to heal and thrive.

7. **Accountability**

Giving people you trust permission to speak into your life is a powerful way to help you set and maintain healthy boundaries. Some people can create boundaries only with the strength and guidance of a support group, which is fine. You need to surround yourself with people who will help uphold your boundaries, not demolish or disrespect them.

8. **Consequences**

Laws, punishments, and other consequences are all forms of boundary setting. When someone experiences the negative repercussions of their actions, they will most likely avoid repeating those actions. Communicating the consequences of overstepping your boundaries lets others know your seriousness.

REFLECTION

*Which of the eight forms of boundaries do you
struggle with the most? Why?*

*In what ways can you continue to grow and improve
in setting healthy boundaries?*

BRAIN DRAIN

Use this page to jot down any thoughts or feelings that might be taking up space in your mind this week.

Things to Do

Date: _____

○ ....
○ ....
○ ....

Date: _____

○ ....
○ ....
○ ....
○ ....

Date: _____

○ ....
○ ....
○ ....

Date: _____

○ ....
○ ....
○ ....
○ ....

Date: _____

○ ....
○ ....
○ ....
○ ....

Date: _____

○ ....
○ ....
○ ....
○ ....

Date: _____

○ ....
○ ....
○ ....
○ ....

Week 19
HANDLING HOSTILITY TOWARD BOUNDARIES

Don't befriend angry people or associate with hot-tempered people, or you will learn to be like them and endanger your soul.

—*Proverbs 22:24–25*

In some cultures, saying no to one's parents can actually be met with immense pushback—perhaps even punishment. People who have experienced this kind of upbringing tend to associate boundary setting with feelings of shame, guilt, or fear.

If you are dealing with someone who might be hostile toward your boundaries, it is best to mentally prepare for possible backlash. You might even need proper accountability to remain firm in your boundaries. Find a community, a counselor, or a friend who affirms and supports your boundaries. Practicing your nos in a safe and respectful environment will help prepare you for tougher confrontations.

Let's Pray Together

Dear heavenly Father, thank you for setting the precedent for healthy boundaries. You intended for us to live joyful and boundary-ful lives in community, respecting one another in reverence to you. Please protect and encourage me as I go out and apply what I've learned. May you also continue to teach me how to say no, when to say yes, and, ultimately, how to take full responsibility for my life. In Jesus's name, amen.

Recognizing Boundary Emotions

Circle the emotions you feel when others push back on your boundaries.

ANGER	CONFUSION	SADNESS	FEAR
Angry	Apprehensive	Apathetic	Afraid
Annoyed	Bewildered	Ashamed	Anxious
Defensive	Confused	Defeated	Cautious
Defiant	Discontent	Depressed	Cowardly
Disturbed	Disoriented	Despairing	Fearful
Exasperated	Distracted	Despondent	Helpless
Exploited	Exhausted	Discouraged	Insecure
Frustrated	Hesitant	Forlorn	Irrational
Furious	Impatient	Heartbroken	Panicked
Hateful	Obligated	Hopeless	Powerless
Hostile	Paralyzed	Hurt	Provoked
Intolerant	Perplexed	Inferior	Resentful
Irritated	Reluctant	Isolated	Shy
Mad	Surprised	Lonely	Skittish
Revengeful	Uncomfortable	Misunderstood	Suspicious
Stubborn	Uneasy	Mournful	Unsafe
Superior	Unsure	Overwhelmed	Worried

Overcoming Fears

Identify three main fears you have regarding boundaries, and describe how you plan to overcome them.

Example: *I fear loss of love if I say no. I will overcome by believing I am already loved by God.*

Fear 1: _____

How I will overcome: _____

_____

_____

_____

Fear 2: _____

How I will overcome: _____

_____

_____

_____

Fear 3: _____

How I will overcome: _____

_____

_____

_____

REFLECTION

Write about an existing relationship in which you need to set proper boundaries and consequences. What boundaries are needed?

What consequences are you willing to live with?

BRAIN DRAIN

Use this page to jot down any thoughts or feelings that might be taking up space in your mind this week.

Things to Do

Date: _____

○ ....
○ ....
○ ....

Date: _____

○ ....
○ ....
○ ....
○ ....

Date: _____

○ ....
○ ....
○ ....
○ ....

Date: _____

○ ....
○ ....
○ ....
○ ....

Date: _____

○ ....
○ ....
○ ....
○ ....

Date: _____

○ ....
○ ....
○ ....
○ ....

Date: _____

○ ....
○ ....
○ ....
○ ....

Week 20
SACRED LIMITS

*Just say a simple, "Yes, I will,"
or "No, I won't." Anything beyond
this is from the evil one.*

—Matthew 5:37

In *The Best Yes*, Lysa TerKeurst quotes Louie Giglio: "Whenever you say yes to something, there is less of you for something else. Make sure your yes is worth the less."* What he means is that your time, energy, and other resources are all limited. Since you can say yes only to a limited number of commitments before you have to cap your schedule, it is okay to assess whether or not you really want to do something before you commit to it. Practice listening to how your body reacts when someone invites you to an event. Many times, our bodies react to the anxiety before our brains can even fully comprehend the pros and cons. Burnout is real, but it is absolutely preventable.

So, whether you are making a commitment out of pride, fear, or obligation, please be encouraged to know that you can be released from the commitment at any time. You are in charge of your own will. It is okay to carve out space for yourself to get refueled.

Let's Pray Together

Dear heavenly Father, please empower me to make the difficult decision to protect my time and energy this week. Help me feel more refreshed and at peace rather than anxious or fearful. Give me the courage to cut out plans that drain me so I can say yes to the divine appointments you have for me. When those divine appointments come, open my eyes to recognize them as my best yeses. Please protect my heart and lead me toward the things that glorify you. In Jesus's name, amen.

---

* Lysa TerKeurst, *The Best Yes: Making Wise Decisions in the Midst of Endless Demands* (Nashville, Tenn.: Nelson Books, 2014), 189.

Never is a woman so fulfilled as when she chooses to underwhelm her schedule so she can let God overwhelm her soul.

–LYSA TERKEURST, *THE BEST YES*

Giving a Graceful No

1. **Be direct and respectful.** "I appreciate your invitation, but unfortunately, I won't be able to commit to that at this time. Thank you for understanding."

2. **Offer an alternative.** "I'm honored you thought of me for this project. Unfortunately, my schedule is quite full right now. Is there a later time or another way I can contribute in the future?"

3. **Express gratitude.** "Thank you so much for considering me. I have to decline at this time, but I truly appreciate the opportunity. Let's keep in touch for future possibilities."

4. **Be honest and brief.** "I need to prioritize some personal commitments right now, so I won't be able to take on any additional tasks. Thanks for your understanding."

5. **Acknowledge the request.** "I've considered your request, and unfortunately, I won't be able to participate. I appreciate your understanding on this matter.

6. **Use polite language.** "Please understand that I need to decline this time. I appreciate the opportunity and hope we can work together in the future."

7. **Express regret.** "It's with regret that I have to decline your invitation. I truly wish I could participate, and I hope our paths cross again in the future."

Your Best Yes

Jot down a list of opportunities you have turned down and the things you were able to fill your time with instead.

WHAT YOU LAID DOWN	WHAT YOU PICKED UP
1.	1. ....
....	....
....	....
2.	2. ....
....	....
....	....
3.	3. ....
....	....
....	....
4.	4. ....
....	....
....	....
5.	5. ....
....	....
....	....

REFLECTION

Name a current commitment that is giving you anxiety. Did you agree to this commitment out of pride, fear, or obligation?

How will you be kinder to yourself moving forward?

BRAIN DRAIN

Use this page to jot down any thoughts or feelings that might be taking up space in your mind this week.

Things to Do

Date: _____

○ ....
○ ....
○ ....

Date: _____

○ ....
○ ....
○ ....
○ ....

Date: _____

○ ....
○ ....
○ ....

Date: _____

○ ....
○ ....
○ ....
○ ....

Date: _____

○ ....
○ ....
○ ....
○ ....

Date: _____

○ ....
○ ....
○ ....
○ ....

Date: _____

○ ....
○ ....
○ ....
○ ....

Week 21
SURRENDER AND SELF-CONTROL

God has not given us a spirit of fear and timidity,
but of power, love, and self-discipline.

—2 Timothy 1:7

As humans, it is in our nature to want order, predictability, and control. That is precisely why the concept of surrender can be so hard to grasp. When situations become chaotic, the last thing we want to do is to give up control. This innate urge to stay in the driver's seat can be overwhelming. However, what if there could be a more qualified driver sitting next to you?

If you are going through a season of trial right now, try to imagine this: You are driving down a road with a dangerously low gas tank during a winter storm. Now, next to you sits the person who actually designed that road. He knows it inside out and has the skills to navigate it better than anyone else. He sees that you are exhausted and overwhelmed, and he is offering to help you get to where you want to go. This person is Jesus.

Surrendering your life to Christ means trusting him to lead you to a place that is even better than you imagined. It is neither weak to surrender nor foolish to have self-control. Choosing to surrender to Jesus shows your spiritual growth and humility, and exerting self-control shows your maturity and confidence in him.

Let's Pray Together

Dear heavenly Father, thank you for showing me a better way to live. Thank you for teaching me what it means to have healthy boundaries and for walking with me as I absorb the good and unlearn the bad. I pray for your protection, peace, and guidance as I practice surrender and self-control. May these boundary-setting skills help me become more like Christ. In Jesus's name, amen.

When we surrender
our toughest days
to the Lord, we can
exchange our anxiety
for his peace.

Reassurances

Put a star next to each reassurance you needed to hear as a child.
Then say each one aloud to yourself.

___ I see you.

___ I love you.

___ I believe you.

___ I believe in you.

___ I accept you.

___ I will take care of you.

___ I won't give up on you.

___ I won't leave you.

___ I'm with you.

___ I care about you.

___ It is okay to feel sad.

___ It is okay to feel angry.

___ It is okay to be loud.

___ It is okay to be messy.

___ It is okay to not know what to do.

___ It is okay to go at your own pace.

___ It is okay to look different.

___ It is okay to think differently.

___ It is okay to stand up for what you want/need/ believe in.

___ It is okay to fail.

___ You are safe.

___ You are worthy.

___ You are good.

___ You are needed.

___ You are wanted.

___ You are a child of God.

___ You are loved.

___ You are important.

___ You are smart.

___ You are capable.

REFLECTION

Think of an important decision you had to make recently.
Did you seek God's guidance? How did that influence the outcome?

Share about a time when surrendering to God's plan during a
challenging experience brought unexpected blessings or insights.

BRAIN DRAIN

Use this page to jot down any thoughts or feelings that might be taking up space in your mind this week.

Things to Do

Date: _____

○ ....

○ ....

○ ....

Date: _____

○ ....

○ ....

○ ....

○ ....

Date: _____

○ ....

○ ....

○ ....

Date: _____

○ ....

○ ....

○ ....

○ ....

Date: _____

○ ....

○ ....

○ ....

Date: _____

○ ....

○ ....

○ ....

○ ....

Date: _____

○ ....

○ ....

○ ....

○ ....

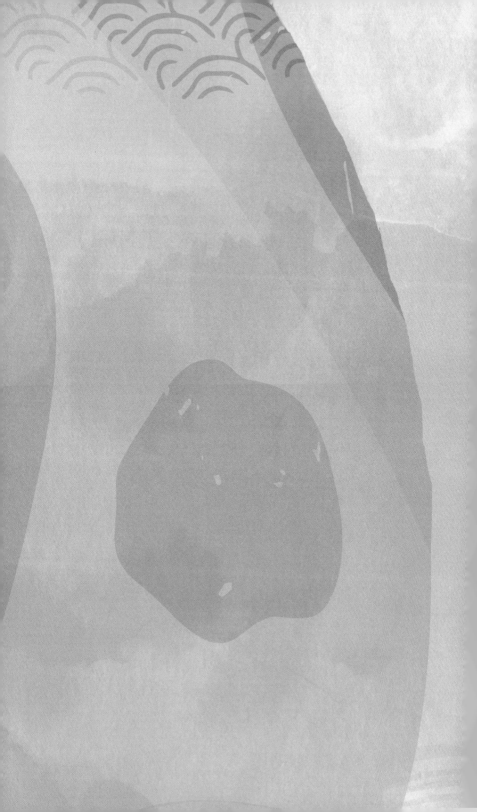

GRATEFULNESS

Week 22
GRATEFULNESS WINS

*Godliness with contentment is
great gain. For we brought nothing into the
world, and we can take nothing out of it.*

— *1 Timothy 6:6–7, NIV*

Gratefulness is a priceless skill to have. It is the ability to feel fulfilled and content even during seasons of extreme lack. Gratefulness, or contentment, is mentioned several times in the Bible—notably in the apostle Paul's letter to his younger disciple Timothy. Paul told Timothy that many people "have an unhealthy interest in controversies" and are constantly getting wrapped up in petty issues. He explained that these are the people "who have been robbed of the truth" and who believe in God only because they want God to bless them financially. Paul ended his point by saying that we can be content because "we brought nothing into the world, and we can take nothing out of it" (1 Timothy 6:4-5, 7, NIV).

Here is the good news: God does not expect you to put on a forced smile when you are crumbling on the inside. He wants you to be completely transparent with him, even when you are angry or confused about why certain things are happening to you. Once you acknowledge your true feelings and bring them before the Lord, he will give you the power to ground them in truth. Here are those truths:

1. **God's love—not health, wealth, or happiness—should be the foundation of your life.**

2. **Even when all else fails, God will never fail you.**

3. **With God, there is always a greater purpose to your pain, and pain does not have the last word.**

Let's Pray Together

Dear heavenly Father, thank you for being my rock amid the storm. I want you to be the unshakable foundation of my life so I can move forward with purpose and confidence. Help me hold on to you as the source of my contentment. Thank you that when you are by my side, there is always a reason to be grateful. In Jesus's name, amen.

Fill in the Blanks

Example: *Gratefulness helps me become happier because it reminds me of everything I already have.*

Gratefulness helps me become _____

because _____

_____

_____

Gratefulness helps me become _____

because _____

_____

_____

Gratefulness helps me become _____

because _____

_____

_____

Joys in the Now

What are you grateful for this week?
Draw or write out your answers below.

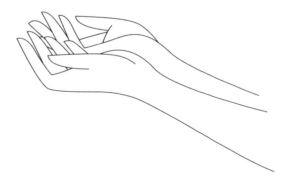

REFLECTION

What do you need to let go of in order to be more grateful?

Share a small, seemingly insignificant moment that brought you joy recently. How does acknowledging moments like this one enhance your gratitude?

BRAIN DRAIN

Use this page to jot down any thoughts or feelings that might be taking up space in your mind this week.

Things to Do

Date: _____

○ ....

○ ....

○ ....

Date: _____

○ ....

○ ....

○ ....

○ ....

Date: _____

○ ....

○ ....

○ ....

○ ....

Date: _____

○ ....

○ ....

○ ....

○ ....

Date: _____

○ ....

○ ....

○ ....

○ ....

Date: _____

○ ....

○ ....

○ ....

○ ....

Date: _____

○ ....

○ ....

○ ....

○ ....

Week 23
THE FREEDOM OF GRATEFULNESS

*What is causing the quarrels and fights among you?
Don't they come from the evil desires at war within
you? You want what you don't have, so you scheme
and kill to get it. You are jealous of what others have,
but you can't get it, so you fight and wage war to
take it away from them. Yet you don't have what you
want because you don't ask God for it. And even when
you ask, you don't get it because your motives are all
wrong—you want only what will give you pleasure.*

—James 4:1–3

In order to truly adopt a grateful attitude, we must be aware of our own insecurities, needs, and fears. Because when we neglect our innermost thoughts, we're likely to experience discontentment. Perhaps the opposite of gratefulness is entitlement. We're certainly entitled to things that belong to us, such as our freedom, opinions, and values. However, the problem is that people often feel entitled to things that do not belong to them, as we see in displays of the spirit of envy. We may also feel the sting of others' success when we fear that there are not enough resources to go around. This is a common case of the scarcity mindset.

When we learn more about our thoughts through prayer, research, and reflection, we will find it easier to be genuinely happy for others without letting their success affect our own sense of worth. Adopting a grateful perspective sets us up for a lifetime of joy and abundance!

Let's Pray Together

Dear heavenly Father, you are so good to me. You promised to be my provider, my great physician, my refuge, and my strength. In you, I can find everything I need. I pray that you will empower me to stop reacting out of fear and start responding out of love. Fill my heart with your peace so that it can overflow with gratitude and love for others.
Teach me how to live in the freedom of gratefulness so I can truly experience the abundant life you planned for me. In Jesus's name, amen.

If we keep
looking for the
next bad thing
to happen, we can
miss out on the
good that we
currently have.

Replacing Envy

What is one way you currently struggle with envy?

Why do you feel envious?

What is the basic fear that drives this envy?

How can you surrender that fear to Jesus this week?

Noting the Origin

*Go back to the very first time you experienced the fear
you wrote about on the previous page. Describe what happened
in detail and how it made you feel.*

REFLECTION

Describe any rituals or practices you have for cultivating gratitude.
How do they shape your overall outlook on life?

What is one thing you're genuinely grateful for today? Why?

BRAIN DRAIN

Use this page to jot down any thoughts or feelings that might be taking up space in your mind this week.

Things to Do

Date: _____

- ○ ....
- ○ ....
- ○ ....

Date: _____

- ○ ....
- ○ ....
- ○ ....
- ○ ....

Date: _____

- ○ ....
- ○ ....
- ○ ....
- ○ ....

Date: _____

- ○ ....
- ○ ....
- ○ ....
- ○ ....

Date: _____

- ○ ....
- ○ ....
- ○ ....
- ○ ....

Date: _____

- ○ ....
- ○ ....
- ○ ....
- ○ ....

Week 24
THE POSTURE OF GRATITUDE

The Lord is my shepherd; I have all that I need. He lets me rest in green meadows; he leads me beside peaceful streams. He renews my strength. He guides me along right paths, bringing honor to his name.

—Psalm 23:1–3

Have you ever considered what the posture of gratitude looks like? Let's practice it right now. First, find a quiet and secluded space. Sit up higher, straighten your back, and take a deep breath. Breathe in through your nose and out through your mouth. Then do it again. Now lean back comfortably in your seat. Don't slouch. Open your hands so that your palms face the ceiling, and lift both your arms as high as you can. When you are ready to read the reflection passage, you can lower your arms.

The posture of gratitude symbolizes childlike faith. Children raise their arms when they want to be held. It is a very powerful picture of trust and total dependence—the kind of faith that truly pleases God. Those who do not yet feel safe in their own skin might have difficulty sustaining the posture of gratitude. It is okay to take it one step at a time. Our bodies tend to tense up as a way to self-soothe when we are uncomfortable, but little by little, we can train our bodies to adopt this posture of gratitude with full abandonment.

Let's Pray Together

Dear heavenly Father, thank you for teaching me how to demonstrate my trust in you through the posture of gratitude. No matter what trauma I've experienced in the past or what difficulties I'm facing right now, remind me that I can always run back into your arms to find peace and comfort. Thank you, Lord. In Jesus's name, amen.

A Psalm of David

(PSALM 23)

The LORD is my shepherd;
I have all that I need.
He lets me rest in green meadows;
he leads me beside peaceful streams.
He renews my strength.
He guides me along right paths,
bringing honor to his name.
Even when I walk
through the darkest valley,
I will not be afraid,
for you are close beside me.
Your rod and your staff
protect and comfort me.
You prepare a feast for me
in the presence of my enemies.
You honor me by anointing my head with oil.
My cup overflows with blessings.
Surely your goodness and unfailing love will pursue me
all the days of my life,
and I will live in the house of the LORD
forever.

Gratitude Cup

*Fill the cup with images or words of what you
are grateful for today.*

REFLECTION

How do you feel while practicing the posture of gratitude?

*In what other circumstances or settings are you
able to practice gratefulness?*

BRAIN DRAIN

Use this page to jot down any thoughts or feelings that might be taking up space in your mind this week.

Things to Do

Date: _____

- ○ ....
- ○ ....
- ○ ....

Date: _____

- ○ ....
- ○ ....
- ○ ....
- ○ ....

Date: _____

- ○ ....
- ○ ....
- ○ ....
- ○ ....

Date: _____

- ○ ....
- ○ ....
- ○ ....
- ○ ....

Date: _____

- ○ ....
- ○ ....
- ○ ....
- ○ ....

Date: _____

- ○ ....
- ○ ....
- ○ ....
- ○ ....

Date: _____

- ○ ....
- ○ ....
- ○ ....
- ○ ....

Week 25

THE CONTAGIOUS MINDSET OF ABUNDANCE

The Kingdom of God is not a matter of what we eat or drink, but of living a life of goodness and peace and joy in the Holy Spirit.

—*Romans 14:17*

We have all heard it said that misery loves company, but a joyful and content spirit can be just as contagious. Instead of tearing others down or making a bad situation even worse, people who approach life with gratitude tend to help others see hope, even when it might seem distant. Goodness and wisdom flow from their mouths, and compassion flows from their hearts. When their eyes are fixed on God, no problem ever seems too big to solve.

Think of all the wonderful things that can happen once your default mindset is gratefulness. You will find it a lot easier to move past momentary struggles and look forward to the future. Your faithful attitude will most likely act as a self-fulfilling prophecy, allowing you to resolve more conflicts than you ever thought possible. The people around you will also be blessed by your Christlike mindset!

Let's Pray Together

Dear heavenly Father, only you know the deepest scars of my past and the strongest yearnings of my heart. I pray that you will heal and strengthen me as I try to live with more gratitude and joy and a deeper sense of fulfillment and abundance. Thank you for being my good shepherd. In Jesus's name, amen.

Cast all
your anxiety
on him

because
he cares for
you.

–1 PETER 5:7, NIV

The Abundance Mindset

List five examples of the scarcity mindset on the left.
Respond with the abundance mindset on the right.

Example: The scarcity mindset says that I don't have enough to be happy. The abundance mindset says that joy can be found in even the smallest blessings.

SCARCITY MINDSET	ABUNDANCE MINDSET
1.	1. ....
2.	2. ....
3.	3. ....
4.	4. ....
5.	5. ....

Have a Spring Roll Party!

A wonderful way to exercise the abundance mindset is to share a meal with others. Spring rolls are one of my favorite community-oriented foods.

SPRING ROLLS

Ingredients

Spring Rolls

Number varies depending on the size of your party.

Lettuce

Fresh basil

Fresh mint

1 cup shrimp

1 pound pork belly

Rice paper

4 cups warm water for dipping rice paper

Dipping Sauce

4 teaspoons fish sauce

¼ cup water

2 tablespoons fresh lime juice

1 clove garlic, minced

2 tablespoons granulated sugar

½ teaspoon garlic chili sauce

3 tablespoons hoisin sauce

1 teaspoon finely chopped peanuts

Instructions

1. Rinse the lettuce and herbs. Set aside.

2. Steam, shell, and devein the shrimp. Set aside.

3. Boil and thinly slice the pork belly. Set aside.

4. Combine all the dipping sauce ingredients. Set aside.

5. Pour the warm water into a large bowl.

6. Gather around the table and enjoy! Start by submerging one piece of rice paper in the warm water so it can soften. Lay it flat on your plate. Fill it with all the ingredients. Fold the sides inward; then tightly roll the wrapper starting at the end with the greens. Dip. Eat. Repeat!

REFLECTION

When was the very first time you experienced a sense of lack?
How did that experience make you feel?

Can you identify patterns in your life when you tend to operate
from a scarcity mindset? What triggers these moments?

BRAIN DRAIN

*Use this page to jot down any thoughts or feelings that might
be taking up space in your mind this week.*

Things to Do

Date: _____

○ ....

○ ....

○ ....

Date: _____

○ ....

○ ....

○ ....

○ ....

Date: _____

○ ....

○ ....

○ ....

○ ....

Date: _____

○ ....

○ ....

○ ....

○ ....

Date: _____

○ ....

○ ....

○ ....

○ ....

Date: _____

○ ....

○ ....

○ ....

○ ....

Date: _____

○ ....

○ ....

○ ....

○ ....

PEACE

Week 26
PEACE IN CHAOS

Don't worry about anything; instead, pray about everything. Tell God what you need, and thank him for all he has done. Then you will experience God's peace, which exceeds anything we can understand. His peace will guard your hearts and minds as you live in Christ Jesus.

—Philippians 4:6–7

The world says that the farther away we are from our problems, the more at peace we will be. Unfortunately, many of us cannot afford to escape from our problems. Sometimes there is no other option than to simply go through the sorrows and chaos. In these moments, we may realize that God does not always calm the storms around us but he always walks through them with us. He becomes our peace. And the peace that he provides allows us to be comforted right in the middle of the storm. This God-given peace carries with it a freedom so liberating that it leaves no room to worry about the disturbances around us. No matter how bad our circumstances may be, we can still have a deep sense of peace, knowing that our heavenly Father is right here with us and that the suffering is nothing compared with the eternal joy set before us.

Let's Pray Together

Dear heavenly Father, thank you for blessing me with your very own presence. Sometimes I focus on my problems so much that they overshadow everything else, but I pray that you will steer my focus away from my problems and turn it back onto you. In Jesus's name, amen.

Peace is not the
absence of chaos;
peace is the presence of
God amid the chaos.

The Peace of God

Write down the things that feel chaotic in your life right now.
May the image below remind you that the peace of God
can exist even amid the trials of life.

REFLECTION

*According to Philippians 4:6–7, what are the practical steps
you can take to accept God's peace?*

How can you be more consistent in practicing these steps?

BRAIN DRAIN

Use this page to jot down any thoughts or feelings that might be taking up space in your mind this week.

Things to Do

Date: _____

○ ....
○ ....
○ ....

Date: _____

○ ....
○ ....
○ ....
○ ....

Date: _____

○ ....
○ ....
○ ....

Date: _____

○ ....
○ ....
○ ....
○ ....

Date: _____

○ ....
○ ....
○ ....
○ ....

Date: _____

○ ....
○ ....
○ ....

Date: _____

○ ....
○ ....
○ ....
○ ....

Date: _____

○ ....
○ ....
○ ....
○ ....

Week 27
CREATING PEACE

*If you want to enjoy life and see many happy days,
keep your tongue from speaking evil and your
lips from telling lies. Turn away from evil and do
good. Search for peace, and work to maintain it.*

— *1 Peter 3:10–11*

When everything seems to be going wrong, the one person you can always count on to be faithful and unchanging is God himself. With God as your constant, you will always have an anchor to peace. Not only has he given you his very own Spirit, but he has also left you with documented wisdom on how to attain peace.

From this week's wise biblical passage, we learn four secrets to attaining peace: (1) don't speak evil, (2) don't tell lies, (3) turn away from evil, and (4) do good. These principles require daily practice and discipline. Although easier said than done, they will eventually pave the way toward a more peaceful and spiritually sound life.

Let's Pray Together

Dear heavenly Father, thank you for allowing me to be enveloped by your profound peace. Thank you that the peace you give is not like what the world gives; it is dependent not on my circumstances but on your unchanging character. Please help me master the four disciplines necessary to sustain this peace. I pray that your presence will surround me in a comforting embrace as I continue to grow in my spiritual disciplines. In Jesus's name, amen.

Book Recommendations

SOUL KEEPING John Ortberg

BE CALM Jill P. Weber

LIFE WITHOUT LACK Dallas Willard

A SHEPHERD LOOKS AT PSALM 23 W. Phillip Keller

BE STILL MY SOUL Elisabeth Elliot

Feel free to add your favorite books below.

Origami Bookmark

Let's make a DIY bookmark for your favorite books.
Cut out the square along the dotted line, and follow the instructions
on pages 239–240 to create your origami bookmark.

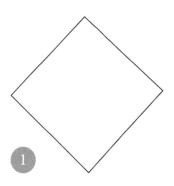

1

Cut out the square pattern
on pages 241-42.

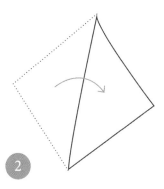

2

Fold the paper diagonally.

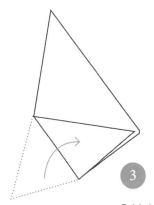

3

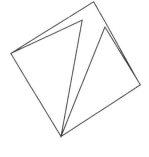

Fold the two wings upward
to create a smaller square.

Origami Bookmark, cont'd.

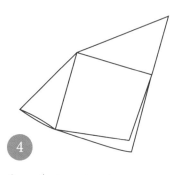

4

Open the two wings to reveal the creases.

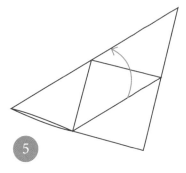

5

Fold the middle flap upward.

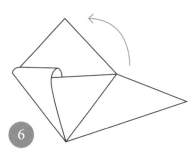

6

Turn the paper so the middle flap points down. Fold the left wing over the crease, and tuck it under the middle flap.

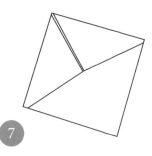

7

Do the same with the right wing. You're done!

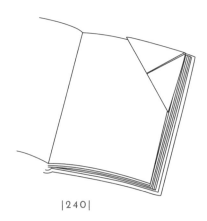

REFLECTION

What is distracting you from having peace in this moment?

What practices can you incorporate to help you cultivate peace during challenging times?

BRAIN DRAIN

Use this page to jot down any thoughts or feelings that might be taking up space in your mind this week.

Things to Do

Date: _____

○ ....
○ ....
○ ....

Date: _____

○ ....
○ ....
○ ....
○ ....

Date: _____

○ ....
○ ....
○ ....
○ ....

Date: _____

○ ....
○ ....
○ ....
○ ....

Date: _____

○ ....
○ ....
○ ....
○ ....

Date: _____

○ ....
○ ....
○ ....
○ ....

Date: _____

○ ....
○ ....
○ ....
○ ....

Week 28
PROTECTING YOUR PEACE

Think about the things of heaven, not the things of earth. For you died to this life, and your real life is hidden with Christ in God. And when Christ, who is your life, is revealed to the whole world, you will share in all his glory.

—*Colossians 3:2–4*

Just like any other valuable asset in your life, peace must be cherished and protected. Sometimes, however, we mistakenly or unintentionally give others the power to take away our peace, only to regret it later on.

If peace is your pursuit at this moment, this is how you can protect it:

1. **Learn your triggers.** Sometimes our anxieties, anger, and stress are triggered by deep-seated trauma, but we remain oblivious to it because we haven't dug deeper. By learning our triggers, we can avoid future conflicts and protect our peace.

2. **Carve out space.** This can look like logging off social media for the day, taking fifteen minutes before bed to pray, or taking a Sabbath once a week. Peace must be prioritized in your schedule.

3. **Draw healthy boundaries.** Be true to your energy levels, and have the foresight to say no to events, opportunities, or situations that may pose a threat to your peace.

Let's Pray Together

Dear heavenly Father, thank you for giving me insight into the areas where I need peace the most. May you strengthen me to make hard decisions to protect my peace. No matter how difficult it is to make time to rest and enjoy your presence, help me protect that sacred time all the more. Remind me of why it is always worth it to spend time with you in solitude. In Jesus's name, amen.

Learn your triggers.
Carve out space
for rest. Draw
healthy boundaries,
and stick to them.

Peaceful Self-Care Ideas

Take a mental health day.

Make time to reflect and give thanks.

Go hiking in nature.

Play an instrument or sing.

Restful Calendar

Plan at least one restful activity each day this week.

S	
M	
T	
W	
T	
F	
S	

REFLECTION

*What day will be your dedicated rest day this week?
How do you plan to rest?*

What activities do you find restful?

BRAIN DRAIN

*Use this page to jot down any thoughts or feelings that might
be taking up space in your mind this week.*

Things to Do

Date: _____

○ ....
○ ....
○ ....

Date: _____

○ ....
○ ....
○ ....
○ ....

Date: _____

○ ....
○ ....
○ ....
○ ....

Date: _____

○ ....
○ ....
○ ....
○ ....

Date: _____

○ ....
○ ....
○ ....
○ ....

Date: _____

○ ....
○ ....
○ ....
○ ....

Date: _____

○ ....
○ ....
○ ....
○ ....

Week 29
PEACE PERSONIFIED

A child is born to us, a son is given to us. The government will rest on his shoulders. And he will be called: Wonderful Counselor, Mighty God, Everlasting Father, Prince of Peace.

—Isaiah 9:6

The peace that God gives us comes through the sacrifice of Jesus. In our reflection verse, the prophet Isaiah explains the different roles of Christ. He is called a child, a son, greater than the government, a counselor, God, a father, and, finally, the Prince of Peace.

A common literary device used in the Bible is to highlight the thing of greatest importance at the end of a list. Of all the incredible names that Jesus goes by, Prince of Peace is apparently worthy of spotlighting, because Jesus is the only way in which we can truly have peace with God. Having this assurance keeps us balanced, focused, grateful, joyful, peaceful, and secure amid anything we might be going through. This unshakable relationship with God—this peace that we have with our Creator—is possible only through our acceptance of Jesus.

Let's Pray Together

Dear heavenly Father, thank you for giving me your one and only Son— the personification of peace himself—to come and live among humanity and to ultimately take my sins on himself and die on my behalf so that I can live in perfect harmony with you. Thank you for your extravagant display of love, sacrifice, and forgiveness. In Jesus's name, amen.

The Four Faces of Peace

You can reflect on the four symbols below as you read the four Gospels: Matthew, Mark, Luke, and John. Matthew (the lion) highlights the kingship of Jesus. Mark (the ox) highlights the servanthood of Jesus. Luke (the man) highlights the humanity of Jesus. Finally, John (the eagle) highlights the deity of Jesus.

Kingship

Servanthood

Humanity

Deity

Memories of Miracles

Describe an instance when Jesus has shown you each of these:

Peace _____

_____

_____

When did it occur? _____

Guidance _____

_____

_____

When did it occur? _____

Discipline _____

_____

_____

When did it occur? _____

Joy _____

_____

_____

When did it occur? _____

Describe the last time you felt hurt.

_____

_____

_____

_____

_____

_____

_____

_____

Now revisit that memory with Jesus in the picture.
Where is he in the room?
What expression do you imagine on his face?

_____

_____

_____

_____

_____

_____

_____

_____

_____

_____

REFLECTION

Between Wonderful Counselor, Mighty God, Everlasting Father,
and Prince of Peace, which role do you most need Jesus
to play in your life right now? Why?

Reflect on a challenging period in your life.
How did your faith in Jesus as the Prince of Peace affect
your ability to navigate that storm?

BRAIN DRAIN

Use this page to jot down any thoughts or feelings that might be taking up space in your mind this week.

Things to Do

Date: _____

○ ....
○ ....
○ ....

Date: _____

○ ....
○ ....
○ ....
○ ....

Date: _____

○ ....
○ ....
○ ....
○ ....

Date: _____

○ ....
○ ....
○ ....
○ ....

Date: _____

○ ....
○ ....
○ ....
○ ....

Date: _____

○ ....
○ ....
○ ....
○ ....

Date: _____

○ ....
○ ....
○ ....
○ ....

Week 30
PEACE BE WITH YOU

Peace I leave with you; my peace I give you. I do not give to you as the world gives. Do not let your hearts be troubled and do not be afraid.

—John 14:27, NIV

We began our transformative journey through this thirty-week devotional by embracing self-acceptance—acknowledging that true peace starts from knowing that we are infinitely worthy in the eyes of our Maker. Along the way, we discovered the power of acceptance and perspective and the significance of our identity as beloved children of God when we accept him as our Lord and Savior.

May your renewed sense of purpose become a guiding force in your life, leading you to establish healthy boundaries that protect your sacred limits. I pray that your daily practice of gratitude will become a consistent source of joy and ultimately help you gain access to God's unshakable, transcendent peace. As you carry these lessons forward, I pray also that your newfound peace can become a balm for wounded hearts and a testament to the transformative power of God's love. Peace be with you, friend.

Let's Pray Together

May the Lord give you peace and a deep sense of abundance. May he walk beside you every single day for the rest of your life. May he bless the work of your hands so that it blesses others and brings him great glory. And may you be continually healed of your pain and sorrows, living the rest of your days the way God intended you to live—with love, joy, peace, patience, kindness, goodness, and all the other sweet-tasting flavors of the fruit of the Spirit. In Jesus's precious name, amen.

Cast your anxiety on Him
because He cares for you.

Abundant Life Takeaways

Fill in the bubbles with three powerful takeaways you remember from these past thirty weeks.

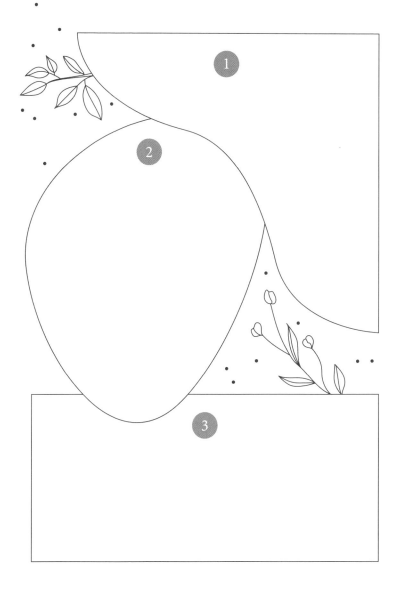

The Path of Peace

Close your eyes, and envision a peaceful path with as many details as you can. Then draw or describe this path below. May this journey be filled with peace and the presence of the Holy Spirit.

Describe your vision for an abundant life, in light of everything you have learned from this devotional journal.

REFLECTION

Look back at the opening exercise on page 9. What has changed in your perspective since then, and how did it change? Do you feel more peaceful, joyful, or faithful in any way?

What practical steps can you take to sustain this new mindset?

BRAIN DRAIN

Use this page to jot down any thoughts or feelings that might be taking up space in your mind this week.

Things to Do

Date: _____

○ ....
○ ....
○ ....

Date: _____

○ ....
○ ....
○ ....
○ ....

Date: _____

○ ....
○ ....
○ ....
○ ....

Date: _____

○ ....
○ ....
○ ....
○ ....

Date: _____

○ ....
○ ....
○ ....
○ ....

Date: _____

○ ....
○ ....
○ ....
○ ....

Date: _____

○ ....
○ ....
○ ....
○ ....

Answer Key

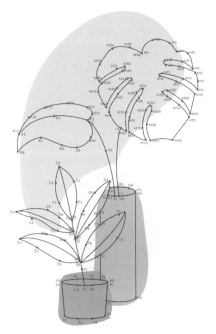

About the Author

Anh Lin is an interior stylist, a content creator, and the author of *Forever Home*. She launched the faith and lifestyle blog called Girl and the Word in 2014, which has since blossomed into a global community of over a million followers across YouTube, Instagram, TikTok, and her cozy online store, TheHoogaShop.com. Anh now lives in a renovated fixer-upper with her husband, their adorable Pembroke Welsh corgi, Ollie, and their lovely daughter, Harper.

May this resource help you live a more joyful and abundant life! This devotional journal is best paired with the Abundant Life guided meditations and soundtrack, both of which are available at TheHoogaShop.com.

The Abundant Life

Copyright © 2021, 2025 by Anh Lin
Illustrations by The Hooga Shop Team copyright © 2025 by Anh Lin
Photographs copyright © 2025 by Anh Lin

Published in the United States by Ink & Willow, an imprint of Random House, a division of Penguin Random House LLC.

INK & WILLOW and colophon are registered trademarks of Penguin Random House LLC.

Interior illustrations: shutterstock.com: Dedraw Studios (pages 4, 5, 12, 20, 28, 36, 44–46, 56, 64, 72, 82, 90, 98, 106, 116, 124, 132, 140, 146, 150, 160, 168, 176, 184, 194, 202, 210, 218, 228, 236, 246, 254, 262); TWINS DESIGN STUDIO (pages 8–9, 13, 21, 29, 33, 37, 47, 57, 61, 65, 73, 83, 87, 91, 99, 107, 114–115, 117, 125, 129, 133, 141, 151, 158, 161, 165, 169, 177, 185, 195, 203, 211, 215, 219, 229, 237, 243, 247, 255, 263); Tanya Purin (endpapers, pages 10–11); Milat_oo (pages 17, 41, 77, 80–81, 111, 147, 251); Net Vector (pages 24, 95, 181, 267); Mystery Kit, half-circle ornaments (pages 50–51); Great Bergens, background (pages 50–51); Great Bergens (pages 25, 53, 69, 121, 137, 155, 173, 189, 192–193, 199, 207, 223, 233, 259); Kristianne Riddle (page 226); R SUHARTONO (pages 103, 227)

Originally self-published in hardcover in slightly different form by the author in 2021.

The quotation on page 38 is taken from Timothy Keller (@timkellernyc), X, December 31, 2013, https://x.com/timkellernyc/status/418142299345133569?lang=en. Used by permission.

The quotation on page 142 is from Thomas Kang, lead pastor of NewStory Church (newstorychurch.com). Used by permission.

Hardback ISBN 978-0-593-60181-5
Ebook ISBN 978-0-593-60182-2

Printed in Malaysia

inkandwillow.com

2 4 6 8 9 7 5 3 1

Cover illustrations: shutterstock.com: Nartco
Book design by Jo Obarowski

Most Ink & Willow books are available at special quantity discounts for bulk purchase for premiums, fundraising, and corporate and educational needs by organizations, churches, and businesses. Special books or book excerpts also can be created to fit specific needs. For details, contact *specialmarketscms@penguinrandomhouse.com*.

2025 Ink & Willow Edition